Scandinavians

NEVER REPEAT GOSSIP

... So listen carefully

by Art Lee

Adventure Publications, Inc.
Cambridge, Minnesota

Dedication

To My Grandkids: Molly, Maddy, Kristian, Eirik, and Micah

Acknowledgments

An extra big "takk" (thanks) to Monica Ahlman of Adventure Publications for her shepherding this book through from start to finish. (The fact that she speaks Norwegian didn't hurt, either—despite all those questions!)

Photo credits

Beltrami County Historical Society: 73 **Bridgette Hallcock/ Northfield Historical Society/Defeat of Jesse James Days:** 59 **Hurtigruten ASA:** 29, 30 **Luther College:** 70

All other photos courtesy of Art Lee.

Special thanks to Jean Edstrom and Berit Hauge Rogers for gracing the cover and the interior footer images.

10 9 8 7 6 5 4 3 2 1

Copyright 2008 by Art Lee
Published by Adventure Publications, Inc.
820 Cleveland Street South
Cambridge, MN 55008
1-800-678-7006
www.adventurepublications.net
All rights reserved.
Printed in U.S.A.
ISBN-13: 978-1-59193-085-3
ISBN-10: 1-59193-085-5

Preface

We inherit reading traits from our parents, or so it seems. Along with eye-colors and ears and nose-shapes and hairlines, there is carryover in reading patterns from parents to their children.

My father and my immigrant grandfather (who could read only Norwegian) were lifetime readers. That's an understatement when applied to my father. Just a couple months short of 90 when he died, he remained The Consummate Reader.

Dad read. Oh, how he read. He forever read. He read hundreds, indeed thousands of books over his long lifetime. And now the kicker: he never read a single novel. He would not read fiction. No way. Never. Whether classics or current-super-best-sellers in fiction—be they *War and Peace*, *Huckleberry Finn* or *Gone With the Wind*—he avoided them all. His rationale was simple; he just wanted to read about real people and real events, thank you.

His idea apparently carried over at least in part to his son; I like many novels, but writing a novel is different. Of my 11 published books, only one is a novel, a story based on events in the 1960s called *Jackpine Savage*. (Somehow it never made the *New York Times* best seller list.) A superb Minnesota novelist, the late Jon Hassler, who reviewed *Savage* kindly in the *Star Tribune*, told me later: "Like any historian you tell the reader what happened. If you were a novelist, you'd bring the reader into the story as it is happening." He's right.

In this book, *Scandinavians Never Gossip*, as well as my previous five books on Scandinavian-America, the prose procedure follows that history format and gets the expected pronouncement: "Yup, these are real stories about real folks and what happened to them." There's nothing made up, nothing artificial. They happened, the way life happens. I hope you enjoy the book (anyway).

P.S. Back to that inherited-reading thing. My son also stubbornly refuses to read fiction. Perhaps this genetic-reading-theory skipped a generation.

–Art Lee

Table of Contents

Looking Differently at the Same Old Neighborhood

"If you've seen one, you've seen 'em all."

"Just observe the sameness. Look around you. Really look! Take time to note the similarities of both the buildings and the general layout of the farmsteads and see the common pattern of the architecture." Those were the closing commands of the hyper-ventilated sociologist speaker at the co-op luncheon in town. The free meal was offered once a year to its patrons. The place was packed.

Gunnar Haugstad, on his way home from the lunch in his new 1947 Ford pickup—mighty tough to buy any new car after the war—was mulling over the speaker's comments as he poked along the gravel road, the dusty machine meandering slowly towards his own homeplace, the farm homesteaded by his Norwegian immigrant grandfather. Way back then the 160 acres had the three precious requirements for any new homesteader: woods, water, and good soil. And 160 acres was a plenty big farm.

Gunnar thought about the speaker's words, considering that odd line about the area architecture. Architecture? He never thought of his place or the neighbors' farmsteads in terms of architecture. Heck, that was just a big fancy word applying to tall, big city buildings far far away. Here in his neck of the woods, here in the upper midwest, here in Scandinavian farm country, you simply built what was needed and no more. You built what you could afford and only afterward hoped that it might look kind of nice. New farm houses meant wooden, two-story clapboard homes built by local self-taught

carpenters using local building supplies, and the lumber likely came from your own woods. And any new house meant using building materials from any old ones torn down. All that could be reused was kept and reused. Save save save. And don't make the new place look too fancy or else the neighbors would think you were puttin' on the dog.

A typical post-WWII American farmstead
. . . and 160 acres was a plenty big farm . . .

Did that speaker suggest that we're a bunch of tight-wads? "Yeah, 'spose he did, but nah, we're just practical," he mumbled to himself. Besides, Gunnar figured that the guy at the mike met his definition of a sociologist, that is a guy who tells you something you already know in language you can't understand. Like the "abbreviated arches" he talked about. Heck, they're just small openings in the attic. Ain't they?

And then there was his crack about "flying buttresses" and "what a wondrous sight they were," but Gunnar thought the guy said "flying buttockses" and agreed that would be a wondrous sight indeed.

Time To Take Another Look

Gunnar was bothered by the guy's assertions. Were they attacks? A smart aleck? Worse, was the guy right about the bland sameness of all the places 'round here? He remembered the guy beside him whispering, "He sess if yew've seen one, yew've seen 'em all, den." Gunnar decided to check it out for himself.

As he puddled along the rutted and sometimes washboard road, Gunnar actually observed buildings and farmsteads for the first time to see for himself the commonality suggested, his head swivel-ing from one side to the other to check it out. Yup, there were the shelter-belts surrounding all the farmsteads, protective growths of tangled shrubs and vines but mainly fat fir trees planted so close together that their branches intertwined to make a forest fortress, a living protective weather-wall to help reduce the icy powers of that cold, bone-chillin' northwest winter wind sweeping across empty fields. Sure, the shelter belts were the same everywhere, but so what? Same with every place having a windmill to get water for the stock tank. So what?

And of course all of the barns were painted red; same red color on the buildings in the barnyard—the corncrib, the grainery, machine shed, pig house, pump house—all barn-red except the chicken coops. They stood out because they were never painted. Never once saw a coat of paint. Almost all were the gray, old-log structures, the now-sagging chicken houses that once were the first homes built by the early settlers a generation or two ago. He remembered his Pa telling him that he remembered as a kid living in that pioneer log home/chicken coop on their place. This made Gunnar believe that his present wood frame house looked mighty darn good, pretty modern, too, even if "the architecture" was almost exactly like all the houses in the area.

The "Good Ol' Days" Are Now

"Ah, the bad ol' days," he muttered to himself, as he thought about some of the first settlers in his area who, even before log homes, lived in dug-outs in the sides of hills, kinda homemade caves for homes. "Kinda modern day Cavemen," he told himself with a laugh. His own boxy farm house was getting to look better all the time. And modern, too; he even had a well and a hand-pump just outside the back door! At the kitchen sink inside was a hand pump too but that pipe went only to the cistern in the cellar. "Yup," he concluded the good-ol'-days' are now. Of course his home and all the houses in the neighborhood were painted white; same color with the two-holer outhouses located not that far from the main dwelling, the tiny biffies half hidden by grapevines and hollyhocks.

Then Gunnar began to study the house roofs, of all things. All the roofs had lightning rods sticking up, each rod with their heavy wires crawling down the back side of the house, ending next to the cellar doors, where the wires were attached to metal rods driven deep into the ground.

Again Gunnar remembered the speaker maintaining that all houses in America are built to fit the local climate. "In the North Country this usually means a brick chimney in the middle of the house," the man said, to help keep the heat in, unlike in the South where the chimneys were built on the outside walls to keep the heat out. Gunnar knew that he and his neighbors wanted to keep the heat in and did so by means of a wood burning, black Monarch stove in the kitchen while the other rooms had space heaters, huge bulky stoves that burned either wood or coal. "Yup, our winters are too cold and our summers too hot. Always in a pickle," he believed.

As for keeping the heat out in the summertime on really hot-hot days? A simple solution: you hung up sheets soaked in water, with some rooms looking like the Monday wash-days, then opened the doors and windows and hoped the wind was blowing through the rooms to cool things off. The standard housing response to summer heat, however, was to build a summer-kitchen, a separate

9

room added to the house-kitchen, with a long, open breezeway in between. It was a useful cool place to do the cooking and to eat hot suppers on hot summer nights; it was also a useful room in the late fall to bake your lefse on that extra cook stove that was fired up just for that purpose.

Geez, Gunnar supposed the guy was also right when he told his audience that the great majority of folks in any region use the same building traditions, the same traditional designs that would be out of place in another part of the country. Is that why we all have front porches? he asked himself. Well, he didn't know about other parts but he sure knew his own territory and he knew that all their houses had big front porches, 'though seldom used, and big front doors, that no family member ever used. The front door entrance was for company, and it didn't open into any inside hallway. Step through the front door and you're in the main house.

Who Uses The Front Door?

Family members used the side door to get in, the one that led into the kitchen, but before opening the door to the kitchen, one first entered into what the locals called "the mud room," a small entry-way where muddy shoes and boots and overshoes were removed and put in a row; also coats and caps and scarves came off there and were hung along a wall of metal hooks. Only then could you go inside the house.

As Gunnar knew well, company alone came in the front door. That usually meant neighbors who had arrived just to visit, or as Gunnar pronounced it, "to wissit." It was good to have neighbors; they depended on each other, needed each other, and were close to each other even if physically their distances were in miles, not yards. In these early post-World War II years, all the neighbors visited regularly back and forth on any day of the week and certainly on Sunday afternoons, but the neighbors always knew enough to leave before chore-time. Milking-time could not be altered, and Gunnar grudgingly accepted the unhappy interpretation that the farmers didn't own the cows; it was the other way around. "Our whole day,

heck, our whole year revolves around those damn cows," he said to himself, and cow-time controls proper visiting time.

Everybody visited. Guests were genuinely welcomed if for no other reason than they broke the boredom of just sitting there waiting for . . . something, anything. Visiting also regularly meant card playing and card playing meant only Whist to Scandinavians like Gunnar, who knew 'bout the game of Bridge but consigned that game only to the snooty folks in town.

Again Gunnar totally agreed that the co-op speaker was also right about Sunday visitors following a regular ritual. It began with a knock on the front door, that welcomed sound required the entire family to get up from wherever they were and all go to the door to meet the company and feign surprise at their arrival. Gunnar could close his eyes and hear the standard lines: "Well, then, what a nice surprise. How are you, then?" "Yah, we were in the neighborhood and thought we'd just drop in for a little while, then." "Let me put on the coffee pot." "Oh no, don't go to all that trouble." "It's no bother." Sometimes three demurrals were proclaimed before the coffee pot could go on.

After the mutual greetings came the grand march into the back parlor, that dark room with the overstuffed furniture—with crocheted doilies on the arms of every chair—the room that the family members used about as often as they came through the front door. The parlor was primarily for company. Well, okay to use it for family Christmas gatherings. The parlor was special. So good "to wissit" in the parlor. Neighbors brought

Neighbors brought news; they were expected to have something interesting to tell, and if lucky, they knew some juicy gossip.

news; they were expected to have something interesting to tell, and if we were lucky, they knew some juicy gossip. If not and/or the conversation began to slowly die, out came the cards, and after that ended, came lunch-time, but called simply "coffee." "Ya da, time for a cuppa coffee then. Sit up to the table."

After the very substantial "coffee" was served—with a variety of open-faced sandwiches, pickles, and two kinds of dessert—and the last final pronouncements made on their three most important subjects in the world: the weather, the church, and the local school, the company leaves amid warm goodbyes and hackneyed admonitions: "Don't take any wooden nickels," and out the front door they go, with an assumption of reciprocity: We've come to visit you, now it's your turn next to come visit us. Understood. Of course. You don't have to call beforehand either. Visiting is a way of life for everybody at any time, any place. Folks will always drop in at any time "to wissit," won't they? Well, won't they? And won't every housewife worth her salt do the fastest tidying-up ever upon hearing that first rap on the door? And won't everything worth grabbing get hidden by tossing it under the cushions of the davenport?

A Way Of Life Never To End?

They will, believed Gunnar. That's the way we do things. Nuthin' will never change. Least he hoped not. Still he wondered about his cousin and his farm on the edge of town. He'd just last Sunday afternoon heard company say that his cousin had sold off the whole kit-and-kaboodle, sold the old homestead to some out-of-town builder who planned to turn the whole farm into a sub-division, whatever that was. Gunnar didn't know; he didn't care either.

"Nah, it'll never change," he mumbled as he braked hard, then shifted gears down into gramma-low and turned his pickup into his own half-mile long driveway. But first he stopped and waited to see who was coming down the road. Soon he waved at the driver of a passing panel truck—it was Thor Blecken of "Thor's Radios" in town—but the sign on the van now read "Thor's Radio & Television." Gunnar had heard about television but paid it no mind, indicating that its only change from radio was that instead of just hearing the static, now you could see it, too. "Whose gonna buy that expensive nonsense? Besides, it'll ruin your eyes. Nah, it ain't gonna 'mount to nothin'. Least I hope not. "While Gunnar headed down his own driveway, the van headed down the next driveway over the hill to deliver the very first television set in the neighborhood.

It's So Hard to Unlearn a Language

Miss Tollefson taught first grade in the Rolfsrud Elementary School her entire professional teaching life. She taught only first-graders. Her specialty in teaching was the pre-primer and she was an excellent instructor in teaching three generations of little children how to read. But finally she retired and on the day after she retired, she took her long-saved money and bought what she always had dreamed of owning, a brand new Cadillac car.

She drove her new Cadillac home and parked it in the driveway. That night a severe thunderstorm came and it blew over a big pine tree that had been in her yard and the heavy tree-trunk landed on top of her new car and flattened it! The next morning Miss Tollefson opened her front door, saw the awful sight, and then she said:

"Oh oh oh.
Look and see.
Look and see.
Look and see.
Darn darn darn."

The (Un)expected at a Family Gathering

I just wish she'd hurry up and well,
y' know what I mean

"You better come as soon as you can; she's not supposed to make it through the weekend. (Pause) Yup, that's right; Gramma Sofie is leaving us."

The message to come quickly went out to family members. Gramma Sofie, as she was always called, was 92 years old and dying of congestive heart failure. Gramma Sofie—Sofia Gudren Maakestad—a child of Norwegian immigrants, had outlived her husband Svein by 20 years, as well as all of her siblings. A strong woman. Strong opinions, too.

Gramma Sofie was known for many things, including, positively, her interest in her church work, and less positively her penchant for the directness of her observations as applied to the frailties of others. For example, she regularly told her favorite niece Seri that Seri's fat husband Telford "wuss a no-gooder, den. No ambition. Ya da, dat man of yurss must have alergies, vorst of which iss hiss being alergic to vork. Uff da, yew poor t'ing."

Fat Telford's opinion of Gramma Sofie's lack of fondness for him came out in Telford's reply to the telephone-call saying that Sophie was dying and he and Seri should come quickly: "You sure 'bout that?" asked Telford. "Are you sure she's gonna croak by this weekend? 'Cause I'm busy if she ain't."

The Family Gathers, Some Grudgingly

The kinfolk came, some arriving on Thursday, most on Friday, all there for the imminent demise of Gramma Sofie. Her doctor had earlier told her children: "There's nothing more that can be done for her," and she had been discharged from the hospital and returned to her home, with hospice volunteers arriving regularly to aid the family in her final days.

On Friday afternoon about a dozen family members stood outside her big bedroom and spoke quietly to each other in hushed tones, all except Fat Telford who wondered rather loudly if she was really gonna die by Saturday night because he had driven a hundred miles to get there and had already made plans for Sunday night and said he needed to get back home. He wanted assurances she'd soon be gone. "She's a tough ol' bat, y' know." The stony, chiding looks of the other family members had no effect on Telford who wanted out of there and out of town.

"I wish she'd hurry up and . . . well, ya know what I mean," Telford whined.

By Sunday morning, however, Telford had gained a couple of fellow impatient converts who were equally, if more quietly, displeased that Gramma Sofie was hanging on so long, too long. "I wish she'd hurry up and . . . well, ya know what I mean," Telford whined. "Jeepers, this is costing me big bucks staying in that lousy motel night after night."

Assurance came when late Sunday afternoon the Pastor was called in as the end seemed imminent. Indeed, the entire family moved into the big bedroom to observe the ending, the members sitting silently in a semi-circle around the bed as Pastor Pederson approached Sofie, lying there peacefully, her eyes closed, her wrinkled skin translucent, her bony hands folded over her stomach. Her breathing was labored, the breaths short and uneven. On occasion she opened her eyes briefly but seemed not to recognize anyone or any thing. She appeared to be fading fast. It wouldn't be long.

The End Is Near (?)

Pastor Pederson stood over her, then spoke gently to her, telling her that he would be reading some Bible verses that she knew well and might appreciate hearing them one more time. At this news her eyes opened wide; then soon the eyelids fluttered, then stopped, and closed. The Pastor next leaned over her to whisper the name of a hymn he would then sing softly. Again her eyes opened wide, but this time they showed a mixture of both alarm and recognition. Something odd was going on. Family members all recognized this sudden change in Sofie and looked at each other strangely, all wondering what was happening.

Then it happened. This man, her Pastor, he with his physical presence and familiar voice had made it happen. Gramma Sofie sud-denly sat straight up in her bed and exclaimed: "The Pastor is here! Time to put the coffee pot on!" With that she jumped out of bed and headed for the kitchen where the startled family immediately heard the sounds of cupboard doors banging and pots scraping the top of the cook stove. Then she called out loudly: "Where are the donuts?"

Gramma Sofie lived on two more months. Fat Telford wasn't there for the end, but he was for the funeral.

American Tourists in Norway Ask the Unanswerable

School teachers all operate on the assumption—and regularly tell their students—that there is no such thing as a stupid question. This assumption is severely challenged by the following actual questions by Americans visiting Norway, as reported by www.dagbladet.no and listed in the May 2007 issue of *VIKING* magazine, a publication of Sons of Norway.

1) Is it true that Norwegian women stay pregnant for twelve months so that their children can stand the cold better?

2) When do the fjords close?

3) Are trolls still around? Are they nice or are they mean?

4) When is troll-hunting season?

5) Are the sculptures made from real human bones? *(tourist in Oslo's Vigeland Park)*

6) Do the Vikings live on reservations now?

7) *(Tourist at Ulstein Kloster, a monastery built in the 1200s)* Look at these walls. They're just like Disneyland.

8) *(Tourist, upon seeing a small stuffed seal toy for children)* They even kill the little ones! Isn't that just awful?!

9) *(Tourist, pointing to a wooden troll figure)* Is this a Sami person?

A Bright Night to Remember

... expanding the blessings of modern living

The neighbors began to assemble on the top of the hill, still not really sure of what to expect. Entire farm families began to arrive, all milling about on the high summit, all looking down on the wide valley below, all trying to see where their own farms lay out there somewhere in the darkness. All did not know for sure what would happen that night, but all hoped it would happen anyway.

Gradually the mumbling men and women drifted away from spouses, each forming their own gender group, and each offering opinions as to the anticipated positive outcome that supposedly was to arrive within the hour. But several folks voiced doubts, with Kari Tollufsrud convinced that more bad than good would come out of it, what with all those unsightly wires hanging around the barnyard. "Dey're dangerous; dey'll start buildings on fire for sure, den." However, in the men's circle Kari's husband, Bjørn, told the curious listeners that the biggest benefit arriving tonight would be getting rid of those blame lanterns. "Dey're dangerous; dey're da cause of many fires."

Are We In Danger?

All then looked down the hill at one of those kerosene lanterns coming slowly up the steep incline to join them, the moving light in the hands of Magnus Kirkeby who with the missus and the kids was arriving late to join his neighbors. Magnus was regarded as the neighbor most responsible for this entire event, recently going so far as to volunteer himself and his hired man to work and help the crew as they dug the holes for the poles along his mile-long driveway. And for over a year Magnus had made a nuisance of himself bugging government officials in town to come to their valley and bring the blessings of modern living to his fellow farmers.

Magnus, still huffing and puffing from the arduous uphill walk, had barely time to catch his breath before the basic question was voiced as Orvis Olsen phrased it: "Ya, den, do yew t'ink it vill vork?" To which Magnus retorted, "Of course it will work! It's worked all over the countryside in the northern part of the county—where they got more pull with federal officials than me. The main line's been strung for months now and the feeder wires finally got connected. It'll work, then, you betcha. In five minutes you'll see the results over the whole valley."

The Tensions Of Uncertainty

"In five minutes you'll see the valley go up in flames," whispered Kari Tollefsrud to Mrs. Kleng Swenson. "Oooo, gracious me, I don't believe that," she replied. "My husband says that tonight we're finally gonna catch up with the rest of the country and life will be so much easier. I sure hope he's right. And I sure hope I pushed the right switches in my house before leaving." And then she added, more perplexed than proud: "Do you know that husband of mine got the machine shed and even the pump-house wired?" She stopped and squinted at her time-piece: "Well, jus' two minutes to go."

By this time, pocket watches had come out from their bib-overall pockets and were lying in the rough hands of the anxious men, many having trouble reading the dials in the darkness and so they were holding them up to catch some of the light from the July half-moon shining intermittently between fast-moving clouds. There were brief arguments over whose watch kept the most accurate time but all could agree that any moment now it would happen. It was supposed to happen at the stroke of eight o'clock. As the hour approached, all talking stopped; the hilltop became completely silent.

The Mystery Solved

And then it happened. They saw it happening before them, saw this amazing sight, saw it happen all over the valley. Somewhere someone had thrown a main switch and electricity had suddenly, magically appeared in their valley. They saw the lights on in their own farm homes a mile or more away. They saw yard-lights shining; they saw kitchen lights shining; they saw the pale lights coming through the tiny windows in the barns. They saw a miracle right before their own eyes! And it was not only wonderful, it was breathtaking! The 4th of July fireworks that they had witnessed the previous week in town were not half as exciting, let alone meaningful, as the magic lights in front of them on this night that electricity came to their countryside. Their dreams had come true. A bright night to remember. A man-made wonder.

> *They saw a miracle right before their own eyes! And it was not only wonderful, it was breathtaking!*

Afterward

Those folks there on that hill that special night would never forget it, never miss a later opportunity to relate to others the beautiful shock of seeing all those lights. Many years later they tried to share this extraordinary experience with their grandchildren, but the effect was gone. They saw only the blank, bored childrens' faces which revealed their ho-hum reaction to yet another elderly proclamation on the not-so-good Good-ol'-Days. So what's the big deal? they responded with their eyes. Everybody's got electricity, don't they? Boring subject.

Only the contemporaries of the neighbors-on-the-hill would listen and understand and share their enthusiasm; and only those once-farmers-themselves who carried those kerosene lanterns to the

barns every morning and every night, year after year, would understand completely and share their glory of that moment.

Eventually all of the neighbors-on-the-hill could later smile broadly every time they heard the story of what Kari Tollefsrud did that same night when she got back to her farmhouse, the home she was sure would go up in flames. Upon her return, Kari went back and forth from room to room, switching on and then again and again the light switches in all the rooms, walking deliberately upstairs, downstairs and down to the earth-floor basement. Almost in a daze, she did this switching-on-lights-miracle for over an hour, all the time repeating one single phrase, that summed up for her and many of her generation that true amazement, that banal line that totally reveals the emotion of an extraordinary occurrence: "Isn't that something. ISN'T THAT SOMETHING!"

And it was "something," something indeed wonderful for millions of farm families throughout America. In 1935 the Rural Electrification Administration (regularly referred to as "the REA") was established by the federal government to begin a program to bring electricity to rural areas not served by private public utilities. This ambitious plan would take years, indeed decades to complete. For example, many rural areas would have to wait until the 1950s and even into the '60s before electricity arrived at their remote farms. But when it did finally come, it was a wonderful event. "Let There Be Light." "Isn't that something!"

A Fourth of July Parade

What a sad-looking outfit. A rag-tag bunch of leftovers if ever there was one, or so it seemed. Old Legionnaires marching; well, half-marching, at times more meandering, down Main Street. And they're leading this year's 4th of July Parade?

Small wonder that some young people watching from the curb began to laugh out loud. Such smugness seemed perfectly rational to them because what they were looking at—rather what they thought they saw—were about a dozen old military poops who were pretending to be important. What the young folks saw were some over-the-hill old vets. Too bad. Actually kind of sad; no, not kind of, but really sad. A sad scene for different reasons. No wonder then that even a few older adults in the crowd obviously felt sorry for the men and began to shake their heads at the sight of these fading World War II veterans trying to act so strong and so brave. At the time they appeared to be neither. Few in the big crowd seemed to appreciate who they had been or what they had done for their country . . .

If They Only Knew

Because all these men were once young and so strong and so brave. A half-century ago each one of them had committed acts of ongoing courage and bravery and devotion for their buddies and for their nation, multiple acts amid fierce combat that those many current scoffers along the street could never imagine, let alone believe. The

crowd didn't know. Ignorance is not bliss; it is sad, indeed almost tragic in their not knowing what every one of those now white-haired old men had gone through in WW II. If the laughers only knew, if the head-shakers had just known only one military story about each of those lives now proudly marching—even if not marching well—still marching down the street, still proud, still patriotic, still pleased that they could march at all behind their flag. It would be great for the crowd "if they only knew;" more-

> *. . . it would be simply fair—indeed, uplifting—for every onlooker to have had even a minimal under-standing of the history of just one of those fine, brave men.*

over, it would be simply fair—indeed, uplifting—for every onlooker to have had even a minimal understanding of the history of just one of those fine, brave men. If so, then, every witness to that parade would properly witness before them the heroes they once were—and really still are, regardless. If they only knew . . .

In Their Own Words

But let the veterans tell their own stories in their own—if sanitized—words; let them recount too briefly their own autobiographical sketches as narrowly applied to their time in World War II. Here are only three such representative sketches:

LAVERN TRINRUD "I was born on July 26, 1922, lived on my family's farm, attended a one-room grade school. I graduated from high school in 1941. When WW II erupted later that year, I wanted to enter the military because I felt deeply patriotic. My father was dead set against my desire to join the Armed Forces. I had heard about the ski troops of the elite Tenth Mountain Division and knew that many of the fellows I had competed against in major ski jumping tournaments across the Midwest were in this unit. I wanted to join and wanted to ski! It was a matter of pride. I was accepted. On Dec. 4, 1944, my unit arrived near Naples, Italy; we were moved further north along the coast and sent into battle as a replacement task force unit, and I remained at the front lines until wounded.

"We often stayed in villages as we advanced and would go out from there on patrols as a squad or platoon. The further north we advanced, the heavier the fighting became. By the time we reached Riva Ridge, I began to realize that 'Hey, I might not get out of here alive!' The fighting was fierce and the casualties were high. We found out later that only 30% of the division regiments made it to the top of the ridge. The others became casualties.

"On March 3, 1945, the same day that Torger Tokle (a famous skier from Norway) was killed, my platoon was on patrol and started to draw small arms fire from the rear. This resulted in a quick realization that we had advanced beyond our lines into an area between German positions. At about the same time I suddenly felt like someone had just kicked me real hard in the back of my thigh, and I knew I had been hit. The rest of the platoon had no choice but to leave me there and head for cover. I lay by a stone fence alone for hours while the battle became more intense and the mortars dropped everywhere around me. I was sure I wasn't going to survive. I prayed to God like never before. We lost more than half of our squad that day.

"Finally, after many hours, an Army engineer happened to go past my position. He picked me up and with fighting still going on around us, carried me on his back to safety. I was evacuated to a field hospital in Bologna and then to Naples to another hospital, leaving Italy as WW II ended."

HARLIN NEUMAN "When I was 17 years old, three other fellows and I traveled to take a test for officer's training in the Army Air Corps. I was the only one of the four that passed. After induction, at age 18, I went through rigorous training at Jackson, Mississippi. Believe me, it was hard work but I had a goal in mind to be an aircraft commander, so I put my nose to the grindstone. The day finally came and I was designated as an aircraft commander in the B-17 'Flying Fortress' bomber. The crew included the co-pilot and eight other men.

"Our overseas destination was Sterparone, Italy. The flight across

the Atlantic Ocean and Mediterranean Sea was very tiring but we were young and had a lot of energy and it was one hell of a thrill for a small-town boy. I was 20 years old.

"Our combat flight preparations usually began with a 5 a.m. wake up call, dressing warmly for the low temperatures at altitude, putting on our dog tags, and then strapping on a combat knife and a .45 Colt pistol. Breakfast of powdered eggs, fried Spam, and coffee preceded our pre-flight briefings. We carried survival kits with everything from gold currency to toilet paper.

"We carried six 1,000-pound or twelve 500-pound bombs and ammunition for all of our machine guns. We were happy to get the airplane off the ground at the end of the runway with that big load. Our missions would last five to seven hours and were mostly over the Baltic and eastern Europe. We flew missions to Romania, Bulgaria, Austria, Hungary, Yugoslavia, and southern Germany.

"I flew a total of 24 missions before the war ended. Most missions were the same—fly, get shot at by flak or German fighters, drop the bombs on the target, and get the hell out of there. It was tough watching other planes get shot up or shot down, with casualties of various crew members. The catastrophe for my crew and ship occurred during a mission to hit a railroad marshall yard in a suburb of Vienna. Heavy anti-aircraft fire shot us all to pieces. We were able to fly into northern Hungary near Lake Balaton before I rang the bell indicating everybody should bail out. Unfortunately, the charts were not correct and all of us were not safely behind Russian lines.

(Neuman landed safely but then spent his first hours on his knees with a Russian machine gun pointed at his head.) I landed safely in a tree with two Russians shooting at me all the way to the ground.

"For the next month, under Russian supervision, we walked, sat, rode in Model-A trucks; sat, rode seven days in a freight train car to Bucharest. We were finally flown out by New Zealanders on March 20, 1945. After the war was over, I flew my new airplane back to the U.S. I was discharged April 20, 1946. I was not quite 22 years old."

RAYMOND MOE "During WW II I was a corporal in the 15th Marine Artillery Regiment, activated on Guadalcanal. As we arrived off the coast of Okinawa, the Japanese kamikaze suicide planes attempted to destroy the American fleet. They were not very successful, but they did scare the hell out of us. As our Marines moved into battle, guns were firing from both sides, and it was often hard to decide what was friendly fire and what was enemy fire. Passwords were changed daily, to identify friendly patrols or movement of troops anywhere. We always tried to use passwords with lots of 'L's' because the Japanese pronounced these as 'R's.' The trick also helped identify snipers who tried to lure the Marines into the open with friendly phrases so that our men could be shot.

"The assault on Sugar Loaf Hill began May 12, 1945. The battle was as brutal as any conflict anywhere during the war. Our infantry was repelled numerous times, and sometimes several times per day. For the next ten days it was to be a battle of attack and counterattack along a 900-yard front. Casualties were enormous on both sides. Marine units attacking with 50 to 100 men often returned with only a handful alive and a large number of wounded. Our Marines fought gallantly to the last grenade, the last bullet, and their last ounce of energy during these charges. It was a foregone conclusion that the chance of survival was small. Courage was commonplace and heroic bravery, unselfish leadership, and unwavering dedication were the norm.

> *Courage was commonplace and heroic bravery, unselfish leadership, and unwavering dedication were the norm.*

"After the battle the only thing left standing in the city of Naha was one wall of a sugar factory. There were no trees and no buildings. The battlefield was a rain-soaked, muddy, barren terrain, devoid of life.

"I contracted malaria on Okinawa and for the next 20 years suffered from attacks of fever and shaking chills. I refused to go to the field hospital at the time. I avoided the hospital primarily because the walking wounded and the walking ill were expected to be stretcher bearers for the severely wounded. I saw enough of this on the battle-field without going to where the casualties were all concentrated.

"I was shipped home on a transport ship and it was truly a 'slow boat from China' as it took 30 days to reach the U.S. I had spent three Christmases and two Easters away from home and had wit-nessed some of the worst carnage known to man, all of this before I was 25 years old."

AUTHOR'S ADDITIONS In later interviews with all of the men, it is more than a curious coincidence that when they were asked to describe their combat situations, all used the same line: "It was pretty rough." After that they all wanted to change the subject. No one wanted to talk about it. The interviewer had to pry at length to get even their above recollections. And yet all agreed that they would never forget those experiences—and that their lives would be changed forever. Yet none said they were heroes. The real heroes were the ones who did not make it back.

Asian cultures are notable for their respect for, if not reverence toward, the elderly in their society. Americans might keep that in mind when observing aging Legionnaires leading 4th of July parades.

(A more complete description of the lives of the three vets quoted above—and more—can be found in the book: *The Sun Rose Clear: Stories of WW II* written by this author's friend, Dr. Lowell Peterson. Quotes from his book are used with his permission.)

Seeing the Best of Scenic Norway

Just sit back and enjoy the scenery

We had often heard about the Coastal Voyage from others; we'd read about it, even watched a TV special on this voyage along the Norwegian west coast, a boat trip that starts in Bergen and a week later ends way up at the "top of Norway"—indeed, the northernmost point of continental Europe—at a fishing village way above the Arctic Circle called Kirkeness.

Not incidentally, a few towns vie with each other as to which town is farther north than the other. This argument is in part moot as all these towns note that from their town they can get to the REAL northernmost point, Nord Kap or The North Cape.

The Coastal Voyage Tour, known in Norwegian as Hurtigruten, which roughly translates into "The Hurry-Up Route," an accurate description in that the tour-boat makes thirty-four stops in the six day trip. The Hurtigruten runs every day of the year, understandably with few passengers in the winter months. Although not promoted as an Inland-Passage-Tour, such as the one up the Canadian coast to Alaska, that's what it is. Only briefly does the Hurtigruten ship sail directly into the North Sea; mainly it goes between, and among, the mainland and the thousands upon thousands of islands along the coastline.

A Multi-Purpose Voyage

This Coastal Voyage Trip is far more than a cruise ship for tourists to view the extraordinary scenery along the rugged West Coast of

Ships go daily from Bergen to Norway's northernmost point
. . . a combination tourist-boat, water taxi, freighter, and mailman . . .

Norway. The ship is a combination tourist-boat (there were 600 of us), water "taxi" for local citizens (people got on and off the ship at every stop) and it's part freighter (freight-pallets came wheeling on and off at every port) and mail delivery/pickup business. A multi-tasking "cruise ship." Often the stops were fifteen minutes, allowing only this brief time for folks and supplies to come and go from the boat in a hurry.

As suggested, the scenery along the route is wonderful and at times spectacular, notably the side-trip down the Geiranger Fjord where the narrow water-route runs between high mountains. It also comes as a pleasant surprise, upon arriving at the end of the Geiranger fjord, to see—over 100 miles from the main ocean—these huge cruise ships already there, lying at anchor.

At all times the ships' passengers represent most of Europe and parts of Asia, especially Japan. This variety of nationalities on board is indicated by the fact that all announcements over the PA system are given, in order: Norwegian, English, German, and French. (On the ship we were on in mid-July, the Midnatsol—the Midnight Sun—the Germans far outnumbered any other national group).

Reasons To Go

As far as cruises go, the Hurtigruten is a little different than what the average American tourist might expect. But the level of comfort is familiar, as the accommodations/cabins are entirely adequate; indeed, good. The food and the variety of foods offered are excellent; breakfast and noon lunch are cafeteria style, but the evening meal is served to you—but you have no choices for your dinner (you take what you get; passengers called it "the nightly surprise"); but the main courses were very good. And if you don't like the offerings, you can leave and go to a small deli-bar and order an American hamburger.

Coastal voyage ships also go into Geiranger Fjord
. . . the only 'show' offered is the daytime scenery . . .

Nevertheless, Americans thinking about taking this west-coast voyage should take price into consideration. For example, it's somewhat expensive; a glass of beer on the ship costs $8.00. (Then again, all of Norway is expensive to travel.)

Experienced cruise-ship travelers might also expect non-stop entertainment of the type one finds on Caribbean cruises. Not so on the Hurtigruten. Here, the scenery is the main attraction. (But it is lovely.)

After dinner you have to entertain yourself, but this isn't difficult to do, if you plan ahead. So bring reading material along and use any spare moments to read and sleep. All in all, it's a relaxed trip; an easy tour. Just sit back and enjoy the scenery. (And one can always go "out" at night, as there is a piano player in the bar and a small dance floor.)

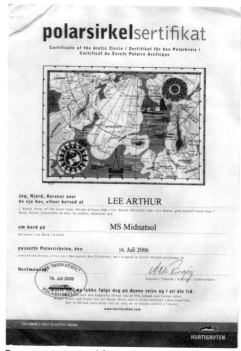

Document received for crossing the Arctic Circle . . . *All in all, it's a relaxed trip; an easy tour* . . .

Folks interested in taking the Hurtigruten Coastal Voyage can book it themselves if they're handy with the internet (www.hurtigruten. com). And your local travel agency can, and will, likely do the legwork for you.

Family Heritage

PARENTS SHOULD BE CAREFUL WHAT THEY WISH FOR

There's an old Hebrew saying: Be careful what you wish for; you may get more than you wanted.

It is common for parents to want their children to become interested in their family's heritage. Whatever that heritage, wherever those ancestors came from, parents hope that their children will want to know more about their inherited culture and appreciate it enough to maintain some of it.

Even the old Testament prophet Isaiah got into the family-history act when he laid out the biblical injunction to "Know ye the rock from which thou wert hewn, the quarry from which thou wert digged." (They phrased it so nicely back then.)

Both my wife, Judy, and I have Scandinavian heritage. She has one grandfather and one grandmother from Norway; her other grandmother was the daughter of Norwegian immigrants. She also has one grandfather who came from Denmark.

I have two grandfathers and one grandmother from Norway. My other grandma was born in the United States in 1866, the daughter of early Norsk immigrants.

Forced Culture

Driving family heritage into kids, let alone making them like it, is not easy. There are no simple answers on how to do it. There are certainly ways not to do it, sure guarantees of resistance and rebellion, sure ways to turn kids off. It can start with the perfectly valid statement that "You are what you eat," so, what logically follows is to feed the kids early on with pure Scandinavian foods, starting with the "purest" of them all: lutefisk. Alas, trying to force lutefisk on children does not work. A platterful of smelly, jiggling, boiled codfish soaked in lye-water has minimal appeal to young appetites (read: none, even to this day). An abysmal, now lifelong failure. Not even empty threats hurled on Christmas Eve—"You're not getting any presents until you eat at least one bite of lutefisk"—worked.

Well, if not foods, perhaps some old-world culture in the form of Scandinavian music might do it, but don't start with the highbrow Edvard Grieg stuff, just pure and simple catchy folk music, the hearty pounding-out-the-rats-under-the-dance-floor rhythms and tunes sounded solidly in Scandinavian polkas and waltzes and schottiches and mazurkas—toe-tapping stuff sure to win them over.

So, on the record player went nostalgic "ol' tyme musik," the kind played to this day by the likes of Leroy Larson and His Scandinavian Ensemble. Great stuff! But alas again, young ears and sounds of a chugging accordion, a grating fiddle, and the oompah, oompahing belching of a fat tuba led to small hands over the ears amid pained looks that told of a needed miracle of some immediate substitute, like maybe the Beatles and their ilk.

Well, if not foods nor music, perhaps some Scandinavian folk-art forms, along with a little language from The Promised Land, might lead to that wished-for interest. So, amid the rosemaled wooden plates on the walls and the hand-carved troll figures lined up on the fireplace mantel, put up the sign by the front door reading VELKOMMEN. Place a plaque by the stove with VÆR SÅ GOD (literally, "be so good," but essentially, "come and eat.") Repeat *ad infinitum* the standard Norwegian- prayer, which begins, "I Jesus navn gaar vi til bord" (in Jesus' name we go to the table). And don't say "Thanks," say "Takk."

Will it work? Nope. When parents see eyes rolling to this forced-culture attempts, it's obviously time to back off. Indeed, they might as well quit; time to hang it up. But they'll be sorry someday!

Rumbles Of Change

While Mom and Dad acquiesced in their presumed failure, there was still that blissful hope that maybe, just maybe, that longed-for interest in things Scandinavian in general and Norwegian in particular might catch on with at least one of our three kids before their folks were old and gray.

And it did happen, long before the change in hair coloring, too, and it happened in ways that at first seemed providential, although more likely it was just plain luck.

Our youngest daughter, Karin, decided as a high school sophomore that she wanted to become a foreign exchange student for one school year. On her own, she contacted the American Foreign Student organization, then did the lengthy paperwork and legwork that would allow her to become an exchange student in France. This process got all the way to the AFS adult representatives coming to our home to interview the parents to determine if their daughter would be a fit American representative so as not to turn around and return home five minutes after landing in Paris.

All seemed to be in order until the first "uh-oh." The most simple requirement was somehow overlooked: age. She was not quite old enough. Maybe next year. Too bad. Honest error. Anyway, it's done. Over with. Forget it.

We did; our daughter did not. The next month she was reading *Seventeen* magazine and saw an article about becoming a Rotary Club Exchange Student, even at age 16.

She contacted the Bemidji Rotary Club and was told the club had never before sponsored an exchange student. She said it was time to start, the Rotary man said maybe and said he would check on it. They checked, and more. They agreed to proceed and she got her OK to proceed, too. Again the paperwork started. Sure enough, by

chance there was a likely opening for one more student in Mexico, a destination that seemed fine with everyone. So buenos-something; she seemed set for a year south of the border.

But oops, then came the second "uh-oh," a last-minute phone call, another setback, another denial. Sorry about that Mexican plan; no spots there after all. Too bad. Sorry. However, we

All seemed to be in order until the first "uh-oh." The most simple requirement was somehow overlooked: age.

do have a last-minute opening by a Rotary Club overseas that has never sponsored an American student before.

Oh, And By The Way, It's In Norway

The mad scrambling was on, this time culminating in her airplane flight to Oslo, but not before a friendly phone call to her first host family in Lena, a little town about an hour north of Oslo. The city is not pronounced as in "Ole and Lena," but "Layna," as in, well, that small village in the county (fylke) of East Toten.

Rotary Clubs require the student to stay with three different host families, three months with each family. Her first Norwegian host family was named Skolseg. The father, Leif, was the banker in Lena, and he had spent a couple of years in Chicago and San Francisco, so he spoke excellent English. The mother, Grethe, knew no English. Their three teenage daughters—Marit, Aud and Randi—had taken some English in school, but they were hardly proficient.

DAUGHTER'S ADVENTURES IN NORWAY BRING CHANGES

An American teenager plunked down in a foreign country who goes off each morning to attend a public school—not knowing 10 words of the language—can prove to be a problem. At best, a challenge.

Our daughter, Karin, reported the ongoing frustration of hearing babbling words by students and teachers all day long, having no

Persistent Rotary exchange student Karin Lee
... *an American teenager plunked down in a foreign country* ...

clue about what was said. Fortunately, however, after each night's middag (supper), Mr. Skolseg worked patiently to help her, starting with the simple grammar basics and progressing slowly from words to phrases to sentences.

The extra tutoring paid off. Still, it took almost two months before Karin declared that one day in October, while sitting in a class, "The light suddenly came on! I knew what the teacher was talking about. What a great feeling!"

After that first breakthrough, it was an easy ride. Soon she was not only talking and reading Norwegian; she was also dreaming in Norwegian. Her parents picked up on her language changes when a phone call to her at Christmas indicated she had acquired a brogue the likes of which her great-grandparents likely had after one year in Amerika.

Home And "Home"

The school year passed quickly, and soon it became time to plan for Karin's return. A surprise wrinkle came from the host family, who suggested that we come over to Norway and escort her home, but not leave until we had spent a couple of weeks in Norway getting acquainted ourselves and seeing the sights. We were invited to stay at the home of the first host family, as a base to tour much of the country. They would show us around.

It was great to have an invitation like that. Passports and airline tickets were acquired and we were on our way, flying directly from Minneapolis to Oslo; we were for the first time in our ancestral land. This visit became more meaningful when we were able to see the homes and farms where our grandparents had once lived, the places from which they had emigrated to America.

There's something especially rewarding in going to the exact spots where our ancestors once lived. We felt as though we had come full circle.

We went to the "Li farm," still called the Li farm, just outside of the small town of Lærdal, just off the Sognefjord. Li (Lee in English) means hillside, and indeed, the Li farm was still there on a hillside, the small farm including almost all of the original farm buildings.

My wife also got to see the farmstead of her grandfather, Amund Syverson (Severson in America) in Gausdal, a scenic area just off from the Gubrandsdal valley and not too far from the small city of Lillehammer. There were no buildings left, however—only the eroded foundations of the original structures on what had been called the Grandlien farm.

Ancestral Surprises

There are many Americans today (and there are now more Norwegian-Americans than there are Norwegians in Norway) who go to Norway and there meet, visit and often stay with their relatives who are citizens there. We regretted that our own families had all become immigrants; there were no relatives back in Norway to meet and greet. My grandfather Lars did have a sister and a brother who stayed in Norway, but neither of them had children.

We also stayed for several days on a large farm (200 acres, which for Norway is huge) just outside of Lena with the second host family with whom our daughter had lived. The farm wife who had also spent time in America fielded many questions about her Severson-family background on the Grandlien farm. The farm wife then stopped, thought long and hard, looked out the window, then turned back. "Actually, you do have a relative. He lives now on the next farm

> *The farm wife then stopped, thought long and hard, looked out the window, then turned back. "Actually, you do have a relative. He lives now on the next farm below us."*

below us. His name is Stinar Grandlien. His grandfather and your grandfather's father were brothers."

'Tis difficult to find something much more coincidental than that. The next day we visited Stinar and Ola Grandlien on their farm. Sure enough, complete with pictures for extra proof, the blood-relationship, albeit distant, was confirmed.

A connection with the Grandliens has led to letter-writing, the exchange of Christmas and birthday gifts, and their son coming to Bemidji to visit us. Moreover, while with a later tour group to Norway, our entire busload of folks were invited to stop at the Grandlien farm for coffee.

CULTURE STAYS FIRM IN SPITE OF DISTANCE

The three of us (my wife, my daughter Karin and myself) returned to Minnesota, leaving behind the land but not the culture of Norway. Our daughter finished her senior year in high school, then chose St. Olaf College in Northfield, Minn., a school where she could continue to use her newly acquired interests and language skills and major in Scandinavian studies. (A major in Scandinavian studies? That was more than we had in mind. What can you do with that?)

The following year she transferred to the University of Minnesota and completed her degree there, then went almost directly to the University of Washington in Seattle to start and eventually finish a master's degree in, of course, Scandinavian studies.

Time To Get Away?

Our daughter then decided it was time to get away not only from things Scandinavian, but also away from the West Coast and the Midwest—time to go to the East Coast, time to go and live in New York City. And she went. She got jobs, none dealing with things Scandinavian—at first. We got to visit her in the Big Apple (great place to visit; sure would not want to live there).

Then came the Scandinavian card again—her job with SAS, Scandinavian Airlines System. With that came her move to an apartment in the Bay Ridge section of Brooklyn, historically once the most Norwegian section in the big city (there is still a Syttende Mai parade in Brooklyn each May 17).

While living in Bay Ridge, she joined a loosely organized group of young people who called themselves Young Norway. The members wanted to maintain and promote their heritage by themselves, definitely not wanting to become part of any long-established organization formed for the same purposes. No Sons of Norway, no Norsemen's Federation for them, their yuppie ilk wanting their Norwegianness arranged by and for their own age group. After all, isn't the average age of the Sons of Norway members 103?

Young Norway had not only young Norwegian-Americans, but also young members from Norway. All well and good, thought her parents, who were finally getting their wish, sort of: heritage had become important to one of their kids.

At one of our daughter's Young Norway gatherings was a young man from Norway named Bjørn Olav Hansen. They met, they dated, they fell in love, and they decided to get married.

This was more than we had in mind.

Norway Beckons

The wedding took place in Bemidji on a hot July day. A small part of Norway came to America for the event, including, of course, the groom's mother. We picked her up at the Minneapolis airport. On

39

the long ride to the North Country, there was one line she said over and over again after glancing out the car window: "But it's so flat!" Compared to Norway, it sure is.

The wedding ceremony would be a combination of wedding customs both American and Norwegian. For example, a fiddler preceded the wedding party down the aisle of First Lutheran Church and afterward fiddled them out again. Two young men, each from a different country, read selected passages from the New Testament, one reading in English, the other in Norwegian.

"More than we had in mind" continued after the nuptials. Indeed, it escalated: the young married couple would be living in Norway. Initially, this decision was based on the practical reason of employment and the timing of their marriage. The groom was an elementary school teacher in the small North Sea town of Grimstad, in southern Norway, about an hour north of Kristiansand. For the groom to get his teaching credentials in order and get a teaching license for American public school employment—and then find a teaching job in some state, all before Sept. 1—would have been difficult. Hence the decision to return to his existing teaching job in Norway.

They did indicate, however, that this first year in Norway would be only temporary. After that, they would return to live in the United States.

It was not to be. One year turned into two, then three, and eventually (at this writing) 17. (Within that time span, they did spend one school year in Seattle before returning to Norway, presumably "for good.")

This was more than we had in mind.

Needed Adjustments

And so we parents adapted and adjusted. Not much else one could do, anyway. Before too long we began to see things differently and to interpret their Norsk residence as a kind of reverse migration. After all, most of our ancestors had originally emigrated from Norway; now one of their descendants was returning to live there.

Hence we have joined the growing number of Americans who have a grown child residing in another country. This long distance makes for difficult family connections. (Thank goodness for e-mail.)

Among the expected changes over the years have been extra flights to Norway. Sometimes the flights there have had considerable motivation, like the birth of a baby. We now have two grandsons in Norway: Kristian, age 15, and Eirik, age 11 (in 2008). It's a long way to go to see one's grandchildren, but it's sure worth it.

As for finally getting grandchildren? Now that's something we've long had in mind.

Exchange student becomes wife, mother in Norway
. . . *that was more then her parents had in mind* . . .

Moving From Georgia to Minnesota

Lars Trulson gives advice to his cousin Truls Larson

—Sell your car. A Southern car will not survive here. Your car will freeze to death before Halloween. Get a used car. If you buy a new car it will look like a used car after driving on our salt-covered roads. Up here an Appaloosa is not a horse, it's a car that made it through three winters.

—We do not have spring in northern Minnesota; it is really late winter. We go from winter to summer in one big scientific swoop. For confirmation, check with your Uncle Sverre who teaches agkromics or is it sniecnence; anyway, he's a prof at Moorhead State. That's on the North Dakota border where the wind blows all the time and when it gets to the Minnesota border, the wind turns around and blows back again the other way.

—You likely think snow is pretty. It ain't. By New Year's Day you'll think you're living in a black-and-white movie. Deep snow don't go away. The reason Northwest Airlines paints its tails red is so they can find the darn things.

—When you pack your bags to come here, bring only one short-sleeved shirt and that's in case you want to fly back home for vacation.

—You will have to change your support for professional sports teams. Doing the tomahawk-chop don't go over here; people will think you're just scraping your windshield. We also got a game called hockey which is played in the winter and in the spring and in the summer and in the fall, so be careful when you get here with your family as hockey coaches will kidnap your children and have them in some program before they even start school.

—As to religion. Well, we have two strong faiths: pro-stadium and anti-stadium. An agnostic is a person who doesn't care where the Vikings play, as long as they play. We all love the Vikings—when they win. If they don't, the solution is simple: fire the coach. We're smart up here.

—We are the only state to have a Fish House Parade in the summertime. Ice fishing is a form of mental torture that shrinks have been unable to cure unless, of course, they're one of them.

—When you go into a tavern and look at that big jar on the shelf behind the bar, do not call the police. There is not a dismembered body in there, it's only a jar of pickled pig's feet. Some people even eat them, especially those who have that common disease here called "Cabin Fever." This rare disease occurs only in those months that have the letter "r" in them.

—In case you may not know:

   1) Beer freezes

   2) A constipated dog is a good dog

   3) In late December, sunrise and sunset are about an hour apart

—But come anyway, not that you'll ever be fully accepted for at least two generations. And get rid of that goofy accent unless you want to become famous and tell everybody you were an extra in "The Dukes of Hazzard."

Culture Shocks for Bemused, Hungry Americans

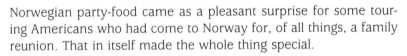

. . . what was stored in those ice chests beside every table?

Norwegian party-food came as a pleasant surprise for some touring Americans who had come to Norway for, of all things, a family reunion. That in itself made the whole thing special.

The reunion was held in southern Norway (Sørland) and about as far south as one can get, with the Lindesness Lighthouse—the very southern point of the nation—just a few miles away. The reunion town was Spangereid, a tiny village on one of the hundreds of fjords poking in from the North Sea, and the location for the official assemblage was a farmstead on the edge of the village.

The 80 acre farm (the land scattered all around the fylke/county) was owned by our son-in-law, Bjørn Hansen; the farm had been in his family for four generations. Bjørn (means Bear) and his wife (our daughter Karin) had offered their summer place as a family reunion destination, an invitation that came as a big surprise. The biggest surprise came when a large number of American family members accepted the invite. Off to Europe!

The Gathering

Some thirty Americans, whose last names were primarily Lee or Larson, agreed to assemble there on the last weekend in July. Prior to that weekend, all the American families had been proper tourists, arriving in Europe a week or two earlier and had dispersed widely to spend time in Germany, France, Denmark, Sweden and Finland.

The culmination of the weekend reunion events for the collective family came on Saturday night with a special party and party-food that we were told beforehand was typical summer dining for Norwegians all over their country. To make it a special party, the neighbors as well as friends from miles away had been invited, too, so that by the time all the folks sat down to eat, there were about a hundred hungry mouths waiting for the food, which may have been routine for the Norwegian locals but a bit different (read: strange) for the Americans.

To accommodate the hungry hundred, a large tent was erected in the back yard, and inside the tent were a dozen rows of chairs around long tables (borrowed from the Community Center), and on each table lay two large "contain-ers" made of tinfoil, in effect large, homemade trays to hold the entree. Also on the tables were platters of thickly-cut bread slices and to spread on the bread were large tubes of mayonnaise. (A few Americans were not that sure that it might not be  toothpaste that would come out of those big tubes when squeezed.) The major foods for the meal were stored in multi-chests at the end of each table, the food iced down until the guests sat down. As for beverages available before, during and after the meal, there were coffee, wine and beer (one big beer keg sat in a big wash-tub of ice at the tent entrance), as well as a variety of pop. (All right, we're in Norway so we'll call it soda water or brus.)

Overnight Guests Arrive

The invited guests—sometimes whole families—began to arrive about 5 p.m., some walking from nearby homes and farms, some arriving by bicycle, and most arriving, of course, by automobile (some Peugots, a few VWs, but mainly Japanese-made cars; alas, just one lonely American Ford Escort there). There were also RVs pulling in, all the owners seeking level ground for parking. Why? What's up? What's happening? The real surprise for the curious Americans was watching (gawking?) at the number of guests who upon arrival immediately began to set up tents, both large and small ones, in the front yard and around the farmhouse. Quizzical looks led to the host explaining: "They're staying overnight. That's quite common in Norway for a late night weekend gathering."

There were good reasons, of course, for their staying overnight, notably for those who had driven many miles to get there, but the major reason—to which the Norwegians would add "of course"—are Norway's strict drinking laws for drivers. They were, and are, draconian. Essentially no alcohol in the bloodstream is tolerated for any Norwegian driver. While some American states (e.g. Minnesota) believe they have toughened their laws by reducing the alcohol tolerance level to under .08%, in Norway it is .02%. That latter figure means that one glass of beer can result in a "drunken driving conviction," which almost always means jail time, loss of one's driver's license for two years, probation, and a fine of one month's gross salary. And more. Also adding to the problem is the lack of enough jails, violators regularly waiting months, if not years, before there's room for the malefactors so that they can finally report to do their required jail time.

Successful Socializing

Gradually, the small crowd around the tent became a large crowd; gradually, the wary Americans stopped eyeing the equally wary Norwegians and although somewhat hesitantly at first, socialization between the two soon led to easy and convivial conversations, despite the obvious language problems. (And the Norwegians knew a lot more English than the Americans knew Norwegian.) If extra translations were required, one of the kids nearby was grabbed in the midst of their play-time for verbal assistance. Most Norsk kids are bilingual; they don't know what the big words mean, they just talk the language that's necessary.

On the far side of the lawn a pick-up soccer game got underway, with plenty of eager players participating, none of them Americans. (Wow! But that soccer ball can really travel hard and fast when booted by a strong-legged, practiced player!)

Finally the word went out for all to stop whatever they were doing and to assemble at the side of the tent. It was time for speeches. You can't have a good social gathering in Norway without some speechifying. The talks were brief; the talks were translated; the talks all dealt with mutual greetings and the need to get further acquainted. To insure fraternization, the order was given that every American at the dinner table had to have one Norwegian sitting beside him/her. Then came the wanted words that even all the Americans could semi-translate: 'VÆR SÅ GOD,' i.e. essentially COME AND EAT!

What's In Those Chests?

By this point the "main course" had been removed from the coolers and poured into buckets; these buckets were filled with bright orange, beady-eyed shrimp, the heaping buckets of shrimp emptied into the tin-foil containers; indeed, the seafood was heaped high on all the tables. And around the edges of the shrimp trays were placed crabs—big crabs, 8-inch wide crabs, hard-shelled crabs to be assaulted with knives and forks and special crab-cracking-pliers. So let the feast begin! Shelling shrimp is not hard; it just takes a while and it's messy. Shelling crabs is hard; it takes a long

> *Dig in! Peel and pull and pick away to get at that wondrous meat, small as each bite may be.*

while and it's messy. But good. It's all good. Sticky, slimy fingers are necessary for this seafood; a mess cannot be avoided. Dig in! Peel and pull and pick away to get at that wondrous meat, small as each bite may be.

The devouring of the foods brought on crowd conviviality that raised the noise level in the tent to the point at which near shouting was required to be heard: "Kan jeg få brød?" "Huh?" "Will you pass the bread?" "Oh, yeah, sure."

No Time For Hurry

It takes a long time to get filled up on just shrimp and crab and bread and øl (beer). No 20-minutes-and-you're-up-and out-a-there. Try an hour, for starters, and some diners required more time than that, but eventually the piles of seafood diminished, or disappeared; eventually *fulle mager* (filled stomachs); eventually it became coffee and brownies time. The dinner was over. In America, this moment tends to include thoughts about leaving, about visiting just a little more before saying your goodbyes and heading

American tourists get ride in "Viking Ship" *. . . a family reunion in Norway made the whole thing special . . .*

home. Not so at this Norwegian outdoor-eating-orgy. So the meal was over and that meant it's time to dance! And dance they did, danced on the lawn far into the night (and at 10:30 it was still light outside; the floodlights on the yard came on at midnight) and folks danced into the wee hours of the morning.

How long did the party last? We don't know. When my wife and I went off to bed at 1:30 a.m., the party was still going strong. Nary a pup-tent had an occupant.

Visiting Americans will always remember their family reunion in Norway. All that food! And the fellowship. And the fun. Perhaps the solution to better international relations anywhere is to have a huge meal of shrimp, crab, bread, and beer. Oh, and tents to sleep in.

The Ironies of Aging

There are some advantages to getting old(er)—not as many as I had once hoped for, but still there's a few there beyond the obvious ones like "senior rates" and no deductions from paychecks taken out for Social Security.

Well, for starters, a man came up to me after I retired and asked the standard question: "How do you like retirement?" I responded: "How do you like Saturdays?" He blinked in wonderment. "'Cause every day is Saturday. Yeah, it's true. It's great! Sure, some Saturdays you have to work, of course, but then you remember that the next day is Saturday, too . . . jo da, all these Saturdays in one week makes for a nice week!"

Then there's the simple pleasure of simple contentment with what you have. It's good to reach that point. Getting old(er) means you've joined up with the multitude of those whose primary ambition involves trying to understand the world rather than change it.

There are a few "disadvantages"—beyond the obvious. You know you've reached some kind of a milestone when people don't bother asking anymore: "And what do you do for a living?" Alas, by ten-plus years into your retirement, you've pretty much lost your former identity, as clearly indicated by a woman who recently approached me, looked hard, scratched her chin, seemed confused before she finally stated more than asked: "Didn't you used to be somebody?"

Aging is like learning a new profession. However, it is not one of your own choosing. And, ironically, aging takes up a extra time, like trying to figure out those many (and confusing) insurance programs and forms-to-fill-out; getting all that legal stuff and bank stuff done; and those unplanned extra visits to the doctors' offices and pharmacies—and which pill(s) on which day. Still, all things considered, getting old(er) is not that bad. You just learn to live with it and do the best you can. It takes time. (So take your meds, say your prayers, keep hope alive.)

Hardly a morality tale but the message is there

Surprises in the Parking Lot

A pattern of behavior emerges each fall as the cold winds begin to blow and the white flakes start dropping endlessly from the sky.

The obvious response to the cold includes folks simply putting on heavy jackets and warmer coats as they proceed through their routines of the day. One such weekend routine for many folks is their driving to church on Sunday mornings and includes parking the car, going inside the warm building, taking off the coats and hanging them on the coat-rack before moving off into the sanctuary for the start of church services.

There is also something regularly left behind in the coat pockets as the owners leave to sit down in their church pews: the keys to the car. Most car keys these days are attached to a small device technically called the "Entry Remote Translator." It's that little gadget held in the hand on which there are buttons to push, notably the one that will open the car-door lock, and not incidentally, when pushed, will also cause the tail lights to flash on and off.

Nowadays there is something new and modern to this winter routine of church attendance: the car thief.

Early last winter at a local church a thief entered the building after the services had started, went to the racks where the coats were hanging, went through the pockets and helped himself to several sets of car keys. The malefactor then went outside to the parking lot

Church parking lot: "the scene of the crime"
... *all involved had learned their lesson* ...

and began pushing buttons and immediately had the added opportunity of choosing the best of several autos whose lights dutifully blinked back at him before he made his selection.

The choice made, he got into the easily stolen vehicle and drove off. At the end of the church services, there were several surprised and unhappy auto owners who could not get into their locked cars, and one owner who had no car there to try to get into. All involved had learned their lesson, one more painfully so than the others.

There is a semi-happy ending in this case that the stolen car, undamaged, was found the next day on a street in south Minneapolis. The owner went down to retrieve it, and the major "cost" to this entire incident was his own embarrassment.

Fine Performance...
But Audience Not
Impressed

Four adult men (who were not intoxicated)
singing loudly

Performers remember special performances usually for their quality. There are exceptions, of course. Our singing group remembers a certain musical presentation not for its quality (hey, we sang well!) but for the audience's reception to the performance.

It was my good fortune to sing with a Bemidji barbershop quartet. We called ourselves The Timbertones, and we sang together for seventeen years. Quartet members, like Scandinavians, are very modest people, hence any hint of success can only be . . . er . . . suggested. This suggestion includes our performing for shows and conventions and meetings and banquets and programs that geographically ranged all the way from Nepewa and Thunder Bay in Canada to gigs in Wisconsin, the Dakotas as well as many towns in Minnesota.

(We also sang each year for my history classes at Bemidji State University when the general topic at the time was turn-of-the-20th century America, the era when barbershop-style singing was most popular nationally. For most of the student listeners, it was the first time that they had ever heard four adult men (who were not intoxicated) singing loudly at the top of their voices.

But back to remembered performances. Along came a request; indeed, one perceived as a grand opportunity for The Timbertones to sing for a big state convention to be held at this fancy resort near Brainerd. For us this was Big Time; it was not any local PTA audience of 13 dyspeptic parents waiting impatiently for the Principal to stop talking so they could go home. (PTA seemed to stand for "Pa Tags Along" or "Pick Teachers Apart." But I digress.) Nosiree, sir, this Brainerd audience would be big and as posh as the posh resort that was hosting and pampering this enclave of special Minnesotans (some were famous; a few were infamous) who were convening to do . . . whatever needs to be done at their annual July get-together . . .

Off To "Big Time"

On our drive down to Brainerd (Bemidji considers Brainerd "down South"), we chose to make a pit-stop at Pine River. We walked into the local Legion Club, maneuvered our way to the bar and there belted out a song that startled even the pinochle players in the back room. When we ended the tune, the place erupted in shouts and hoots and raucous applause—followed by multi-orders to "Give

A barbershop quartet, "The Timbertones"
. . . *song ends to applause and "Give them guys a drink".* . .

them guys a drink!" Soon another song; another grand ovation; another drink. This might have gone on 'til midnight—but we left soon for the Big Time.

This enthusiastic reception of the Legion Club audience is noteworthy as there would soon be a contrasting reception when we got to the fancy resort and the convention crowd there. Upon our arrival, we walked inside, maneuvered our way through the fancy-dressed crowd to the fancy bar, and there again we belted out the same song we sang back in Pine River. When we ended it this time, however, the place was silent. Not a sound. Not one hand-clap, not one cheer, not one grudging assertion of any alleged musical accomplishment, let alone any voice offering to buy a drink. Indeed, a few couples got up, left their own drinks, and moved through the doors to another room. We kinda figured out right about then that it was going to be a long night.

"Alone" In Brainerd

That evening the banquet was served to the honored guests by waiting and watchful servers moving with alacrity at any bid for their services. The food may have been great; we didn't know; we didn't get any. Like poor peasants, we were shuffled off to a side room to wait and told to stay there until we were summoned to perform for the masters.

Finally the summons came and we moved inside the large dining area and shuffled quietly along the wall and up to the stage where the

Caricature of Timbertone members
. . . Hank Rossiter, Bill Bender, Art Lee, Felix Spooner

M.C.—in a snitzy tux, no less—gave some announcements, tried to tell some lame jokes, and then in his stentorian voice proclaimed: "And now ladies and gentlemen, for your entertainment tonight, a barbershop quartet from Bemidji, THE TIMBERTONES!"

At this we bounded on stage, moved quickly to the mike, and came on strong with The Big Barbershop Sound in our Big Opener, a song simply called

"HELLO-HELLO," heretofore a great crowd-pleaser that had never failed us—until that night. At song's ending, there was at best a faint smattering of applause, hardly perceptible.

Then for our second number we came on with a melodic warhorse that even this audience would recognize and maybe even sing along with us: "Wait 'Til The Sun Shines, Nellie." Alas, the sun was not shining at that moment on The Timbertones. After the last chord, a tiny pitter-patter was offered up by the embalmed throng.

So then it seemed a time for a joke, a good story told by one of the best storytellers Bemidji has ever had, Henry Rossiter (who also sang wonderful tenor). Henry is a funny man who tells funny stories wonderfully well and was wonderfully received—until that night. His story was good; the timing was fine; the punch-line was perfect—but nobody laughed.

(Henry's story?: "Hey, I went to my class reunion last weekend and this guy came up to me and said, 'Gee, Charlie, have you changed! You've gotten fat, you're losing your hair, and you finally changed your nerdy glasses. Geez, Charlie, have you changed!' I said, 'My name's not Charlie,' to which he replied, 'Aha! Changed your name, too.'")

Whatever, Henry turned back to the three of us with a look on his face of "HELP!," and the signal for his backup (me) to give it a try. So I laid on them my imitation of President Calvin Coolidge (who didn't talk; he quacked) and the famous story that began with a tourist in the White House asking President Coolidge: "How many people work in the White House, Mr. Coolidge?" His terse answer: "About half of them." In our audience, not a half of a half of them laughed (did they get it?); actually there was only one faint giggle.

Time To Go "Highbrow"

Then Felix Spooner whispered a suggestion to try our "high brow" song, the Quartet Number from Verdi's RIGOLETTO. So an opera piece we performed, of course with changed lyrics, along with some choreography. Musically, it was challenging, but not half as challenging as trying to entertain the finery'd folks lolling in their soft cushioned chairs. They didn't like RIGOLETTO either.

Anothered whispered suggestion by our bass, Bill Bender, who had the good sense to size up the situation and state the solution accurately: "Let's get outta here." We did, but out of plain orneriness, we were not going to leave until we laid one final number on them, and if they didn't like it—and we figured they wouldn't—well, we did like it very much and we'd enjoy it again ourselves, and so we closed off with "German Band," a song made up by the four of us in a car while driving home to Bemidji from Duluth after doing a show there. We thought the tag on this particular song was magnificent!

This enthusiasm was not shared. There was some minor applause after this last song, but we guessed they were applauding less for our musical rendition than for the fact that we were leaving the stage for good. Yup, a tough audience.

Who were the bored half-listeners who apparently disdained barbershop music? It was the Annual Convention of Minnesota Attorneys.

And who was this audience? What was this big-time convention all about? Who were the bored half-listeners who apparently disdained barbershop music? It was the Annual Convention of Minnesota Attorneys.

Not Over 'Til It's Over

Alas, this disaster did not end that night. A month went by and the Attorneys had not yet paid our fee! Our phone call requesting payment led to their trying to re-negotiate the original price! No way! Result: We told them to either pay the fee—or else—(what lovely irony follows)—we threatened that we would hire an attorney and take them to Small Claims Court and there ask for double our initial fee! They paid.

Ahhh, strange about what strange things performers remember.

Barroom Philosopher Knows
He Doesn't Know

Nels Kjendalen, fat and fiftyish, spent a lot of time in the tavern. His farm neighbors clucked that the bar-room was his second home, but Nels' tavern-time was different in that after three beers, or midnight, which ever came first, he would start to philosophize at great length.

Nels may have been intellectually profound in his ramblings but no one was quite sure, as the listeners could not understand him, but people pretended to understand and nodded their heads at all that he said, just to be nice. Nels called his ramblings "synoptic syllogisms"; the listeners called it "deep doo-doo."

Whatever, Nels left them perplexed. Sample: "I know nothing and because I know that I know nothing, I know something." Heads nodded, mostly in agreement with his first three words. It got worse: "I don't know what I don't know. If you think about that, that's a frightening thought." Heads nodded; none seemed frightened.

But then the stretch of stretches came: "Most people don't know that they don't know that they don't know." Heads nodded; eyes rolled.

Most people knew to avoid sitting next to Nels Kjendalen in the tavern.

The Need for a Norwegian-American Mafia

Such ignominy; such sadness; such a mess. Norwegian-Americans have a problem: No national recognition. Not even much state recognition for their own kind. Consider, taking just one sad example, the town of Northfield, Minnesota, a true bastion of Norwegianess—with Saint Olaf College—but what and who does Northfield recognize each year? A famous Norwegian-American? Nope, the infamous Jesse James. With "Jesse James Days" no less. They recognize a crook, an outlaw, a bank robber. What a screwy outfit in that town.

Why don't they celebrate perhaps Hjalmar Peterson? Hold "Hjalmar Peterson Days!" But no, 'cause Hjalmar was not a notorious bank robber, that's why. Too bad 'cause Hjalmar was special[1]—but alas, no crook, no gun, no mayhem—and no recognition.

Norwegians have never had any famous bank robbers. Even worse, they never had any good ol' solid Mafia Families. That's what's needed for our ethnic group to to be known and famous: A Norwegian-American Mafia!

The Knute Svensen Clan

Everyone knows about the Carlos Gambino Family. Why not the Ole Torkelson Family? Or the Knute Svensen Clan? And the Anders Nordlie Syndicate? All right, not likely to happen, considering there were no such cruddy characters. Too bad, sorta, considering the possibilities for fame. Ahhh, fickle fame . . .

Then there's the infamous Mafia figure of Joe (Bananas) Giacoma. If only the Norskies could muscle in there somewhere. How 'bout maybe Truls (Peaches) Johanesson? Or Torlief (Lettuce) Ruspegaarden? And don't forget Eirik (Carrots) Buksegaard. Alas, if only . . .

All Americans know of The Mean Mob headed by Al Capone. Why not The Farmers Co-op Gang headed by Thorvald Johnson? (Because Al Capone cracked heads; Thorvald Johnson cracked walnuts.)

The celebration of "The Defeat of Jesse James Days" in Northfield, MN
. . . *alas, Norwegians have never had any famous bank robbers* . . .

More Non-Norskies

And Northfield isn't satisfied with Jesse alone. Nosiree, sir, they got to add Jesse's nefarious partners, his non-Norskie cohorts, the Younger Brothers. Why can't Jesse have teamed up instead with the Ingebretson Brothers? Or The Kjendalen Twins? The Berg Boys? (Nei/ No, 'cause there ain't no brudders like that.)

Jesse and his nasty Brudders alone share the stage in Northfield's celebration. They dress up like . . . however bank robbers dress up . . .

and ride horses up and down main street and whoop and holler and shoot their guns in the air while thousands of folks on the sidewalks cheer this staged bank robbery. Goody? NO, Goofy.

Solveig And Halvor Days?

The notoriety-nonsense gets worse. Northfield is not alone in singling out bad 'uns and bums to celebrate. A town in Alabama makes a big deal and a bigger weekend with their "Bonnie and Clyde Days." Hoot-ma-toot! Norskie possibilities to cash in on featuring contrarian cohabitating combinations could be elevating for faithful fjord-lovers. Maybe "Solveig and Halvor Days" or "Clara and Øyvind's Shacking-Up Weekend"; perhaps "Myrtle and Knute's All-Weekend 30-30-Shooting-Orgy" Ahhh, the dreams . . .

Boo Hoo. No Nasty Norwegians

But alas and uff da, it's never to be. No national Norsk trouble makers; no big bad boat rockers, so no major movie to be built around

a Norsk Mafia powerful Don (Hey, it could be called "The Trollfather," starring Ulrikke Rømmegrøt and Bjug Bjorstad). No television crime series on HBO featuring the herring-eating-brood of Andreas Rogness, with all 14-family members dressed night or day in their Norwegian too-hot sweaters and all wearing rubber knee-boots. (The show might be called "The Altos," starring Inger Rosedahlen-Fruland and Lars Bjornson-Kittelson-Olson, the TV shows sponsored by Glenwood Lutefisk, Hawley Lefse and The Minneapolis Sons of the Snoose Chewers.) Dream on . . .

Jo-da. However, no point in dreaming. It did not happen; it will not happen. Never no Mafia. No Norsk mug-shots on post office walls. No fame. No infamy. No nuthin'. Nuff to make a good lutefisk lover cry in his aquavit and cancel his subscription to *The Viking* magazine

and throw away his copy of *The Lutefisk Ghetto*. Oh such sadness, especially the last one.

OH DU STORE VERDEN! (Oh, you great big world!)

[1]To the curious: Hjalmar Peterson was an entertainer in the many Scandinavian bars along Minneapolis' Cedar Avenue early in the 20th century, in the bygone days when that street was best known as Snoose Boulevard. Hjalmar took the stage name of Ole Skrutholdt, with his most famous and most requested song being "Nikolina."

A great place to visit, but . . .

Twists and Surprises in Trips Abroad

There are interesting twists for American tourists who travel overseas. Among the top motives for going are to see and learn about these foreign countries, but a twist comes when one ends up learning more about your own country than the countries you visit.

The American traveler abroad cannot help but make comparisons between what one sees and hears there and back home. What one sees and experiences does not necessarily correspond to what one expected. And those pre-thought stereotypes are destroyed.

The Apprehensive Group Arrives

Fourteen of us from Minnesota went on a "Baltic Sea Cruise." The twists and turns were everywhere, starting with geography shifts because this cruise actually began way inland, with the first destination being Moscow—a mighty long way from the Baltic Sea.

Like most overseas trips, the most wearying part is getting there. It's one long, tiring "day" to get to Moscow from Minnesota, Bemidji to Minneapolis to Amsterdam—you've "lost" one day by the time the plane lands in the Netherlands—and you finally arrive bone-weary in the late afternoon in a Moscow airport.

Surprises were everywhere. Moscow does not have one airport; it has four. And while most countries do not require visas, Russia does, and one's visa-numbers had best line up with the ones on the

Russian custom's computer-screen or it's turn-around-right-there and head back home.

Tourists sort of know that Russia is a big country. They also know it's a long way from New York to Los Angeles, what with our four time zones, then they learn that Russia has eleven time zones. It's farther from Moscow to Vladivostok on the Pacific ocean than it is from Moscow to New York across the Atlantic ocean.

> *. . . and then they learn that Russia has eleven time zones.*

All "Greek" To Us

And then there's the Russian alphabet. In much of Europe one can look at the signs on the bulletin boards and often figure out in part what it says, but not so in Russia. Their Cyrillic alphabet is a mystery for almost all Americans, with unknown letters, backward letters and "numbers" all in the same word, e.g. "Cy3 ll*qzh".

Tourists sort of know that Moscow is a big city. But eleven million people!? More than twice the population of all Minnesota in one city! And 157 subway stations? Each station is sort of a special "art gallery," each station having its own decor and art and decorations, as directed when built in the 1930s by Stalin who was quoted as saying that any Moscow subway station is to be "The Poor Man's Palace." And not one mark of graffiti on any Moscow station wall. (New York it ain't.)

Are there many automobiles in Moscow? We weren't sure. There didn't used to be, or so we thought. We learned otherwise. Our hotel was just across the street from Red Square and the Kremlin, with the street going by having eight lanes of cars, with so many wild drivers that trying to cross, even at the stop light (stop lights seem to be viewed as just suggestions to drivers) required both nimbleness of foot and daring. (Later in our tour bus, while sitting in a traffic jam, our guide told our group that even by the year 2000 Moscow did not quite know what the term traffic-jam meant. They learned. Cars everywhere!)

Signs And Sick Jokes

So Communism ended about 1990; by 2005 it was surely enough time to remove all those signs and symbols of the bad old Red days. Not so; not true. On the roofs of some buildings there were still lighted huge red stars at night; on the sides of buildings still the old Hammer-and-Sickle, reminders of the former Soviet Union. The infamous KGB (the dreaded Soviet Secret Police) building is now open to tourists, and

two different guides told us the same then-current Russian joke as we drove by: "The KGB building was once the tallest building in Moscow. Even from the basement you could see Siberia."

There is a bit of irony in the fact that most foreigners visiting Russia want to see not "Today's Russia" but "Old Czarist Russia," the Russia that ended in 1917. Hence in this 21st century that means joining the shuffling crowds traipsing through and oooing and ahhhing at the ostentatious splendors of the Czars' palaces, the ones

in the city and those splendiferous palaces in the countryside; and see the Czarina's palaces, and also their children's palaces. (If nothing else, one can figure out why there was a revolution.) Like one can get "cathedraled out" in old Europe; one can get "palaced out" in old Russia.

Borsch And Balalaikas

And what of the alleged standard Russian foods we associate with the Russians? Only one time was our tour-group served borsch (beet soup), this at a noon-meal in a kind of country-inn outside the city. That dinner, set up just for tourists, produced all the stereotypes of Russian foods, whether fish-soup, crusty brown-black hardbread, tart cole slaw, or the ground-beef patties wrapped in cabbage leaves. And oh yes, on every table was a full bottle of vodka. Between food courses we were entertained by big burly men wearing blouses and high black boots who danced and sang while balalaikas were strummed in the background. Wonderfully entertaining. Scenes right out of Doctor Zhivago.

MAYHEM: All In One Week

On the day we left Moscow there came an English-language newspaper delivered to our hotel room, which included the city's crime statistics for the one week just ended: Murders, 11; assaults, 40; robberies, 292; rape, 6; theft, 1,028; car theft, 57; car accidents, 122; suicides, 22; missing persons, 65; bodies discovered, 89. (We wondered how many in the latter figure had died from too much vodka.)

We had to leave Moscow too soon and fly to Copenhagen, there to board the cruise ship to start the real Baltic Sea part of the tour. (The day after we left our particular Moscow airport, two passenger-planes were blown up less than 15 minutes after leaving that same airport. WHEW!) Anyway, it was on to the old Leningrad and/or the new St. Petersburg (the same city)—where continued twists and surprises continued to impress if not confound American tourists. But no surprise when we joined the hordes of people to shuffle-shuffle-step-step through The Hermitage Art Museum. Still it's one great experience to visit Russia's two biggest cities. Yup, sure great places . . . but wouldn't want to live there . . .

The power of music—in strange ways
The Response(s)

Tom Johnson played trumpet in his high school band. So? No big deal. At least he didn't think so. In his small town and small school band, almost anyone who could hold an instrument could be in the band, even if that person was placed in the last seat of the last row of the last section with the sheet music on the stand ahead of him labeled "Fourth Trumpet."

Tom Johnson played good trumpet. He not only sat in the first row of the section but in the first chair, too. Then again Tom knew that in a band that was not that great, it wasn't that great to be the first-chair trumpet player. And besides, sports were more important than music.

Tom Johnson played good basketball. So? A big deal. At least he thought so. Certainly the townspeople thought so, as they lived and died with the outcomes of the local high school games. Midwest winters were not something to be dreaded and endured, they were seasons looked forward to, cold months to be enjoyed, exciting times because after all, wintertime was The Basketball Season. Life is worth living.

At games in the school gymnasium, the bleachers on both sides were always jammed full with howling spectators. When the band concerts were played from the stage in the same gym, there was little noise from the bleachers because there were not many folks in

the bleachers. The few folding chairs on the gym floor might be half filled with folks, mainly the parents of the band members, along with assorted relatives and loving grandparents, with perhaps a few of the bored, curious townspeople. Almost all came more out of duty and guilt rather than in search of aesthetic pleasures.

Such was the value system of this town, as well as most small communities in the upper Midwest. Accept it. That's the way it was; that's the way it is. A way of life. Basketball over Bach anytime. Well, almost any time.

A Strange Change

Strangely if not miraculously, this value system changed almost instantly for Tom Johnson after one experience, seeing and hearing a touring college band that played a concert in the school gym. His response to this concert changed his life.

Sponsored by both local Lutheran churches, the Luther College Concert Band from Decorah, Iowa, included Tom's town on their winter tour, and because both churches became competitive as to which members could sell the most tickets, both the bleachers and the main floor folding chairs were filled with concert-goers the night of the performance. The combination of advertising, and the near badgering by salespeople to buy a ticket, brought in the big crowd. After all, this was special, this was the CONCERT BAND of Luther College. After all, Luther had the reputation; this was the school that the local pastors not so subtly guided the local high school seniors to attend. Go to a state college or a church college? A no brainer. And which church college? Why Luther College, of course. After all, the local pastors Gunnar Hillestad and Bent Brubakken knew best. After all, both pastors had gone to Luther College.

On the night of the concert, Tom Johnson sat in the top row of the bleachers, slouching with the rest of the starting-five on his basketball team. All wore their letter-jackets; all tried to look bored;

all were bored. But what else is there to do in a small town on a non-game night? Almost everybody in the community was there anyway, and the team members were just following the herd. The thing to do; the place to go. And who knows that maybe it wouldn't be too boring after all.

The starting time arrived. The announcer, Pastor Hillestad, went to the microphone and delivered obligatory thank-yous. He then introduced the Luther College Concert Band, with all the flourish of an Ed McMahon bringing on Johnny Carson. The floor lights went off; the stage lights went on as the front curtains opened swiftly to an imposing sight on stage. Wow! Tom Johnson remembered the oft-repeated line of his own band director: "First through the eyes, and then through the ears." Before him was this impressive sight of 65 young musicians who seemed great before one note had been sounded.

To Tom's eyes came this sea of black, the men dressed in tuxedoes, the women in long black dresses. They all sat at attention and held their instruments straight in front of them. No one moved a muscle. Pure spiff. Then onto the stage came the director who did not walk on, but he bounced on and hopped on to the podium. After one quick bow, he turned back to the band; his arms went up and their instruments came up. Then down came the baton and the trumpets drove home the crisp, opening notes of "The Procession of the Nobles," always a crowd pleaser. So clean! So clear! Such precision! Wow! While most of the audience was impressed, Tom Johnson was overwhelmed. What a band! What showmanship! Cool! And those trumpets! Great!

Could it get any better? For Tom Johnson, it got super- better when the featured soloist was a trumpeter performing flawlessly "The Trumpeter's Lullaby." By this point Tom Johnson was in such awe that he felt paralyzed and he could not join in the wild applause when each piece ended. This superb concert band's final number was the powerful "Stars and Stripes Forever," and just prior to the second ending of the chorus, the whole trumpet section arose from their chairs in the back, marched in order to the front of the stage, and in one long line they blasted out that last chorus with such

force and command—and one trumpeter was an octave above he rest—as to make the hairs rise on Tom Johnson's arms. A minor miracle had happened. He believed at that moment that more

A minor miracle had happened. He believed at that moment that more than anything, he wanted to play trumpet in the Luther College Concert Band.

than anything, he wanted to play trumpet in the Luther College Concert Band. He could do it; he would do it. An instant goal. A realistic dream. Go for it! After all, grownups had always told him to Follow Your Dreams! Now he knew which dream to follow. Ahh, the power of music . . .

Slouching To The End

The school year slouched slowly towards the end, as did the basketball season, the season ending as usual with the tournament- time's eventual sadness amid the annual March Madness. As usual, another "wait'll next year" refrain. And as usual, the season ended with the year's last big snowstorm. Somehow basketball tournaments in the Midwest and snowstorms always seemed to go together.

Graduation came along, finally, and by then most of Tom Johnson's fellow seniors still wrestled with what to do after high school. With a four year athletic scholarship offered to Tom Johnson by the nearby state college, the decision of what to do and where to do it was easy. No problem. Tom Johnson was going to Luther College and play in their Concert Band. Four great years of trumpet-playing ahead! And after that, maybe become a band teacher or maybe get in a military band or maybe play in a big-time dance band. Who knows? Just to think about his musical future made him feel good all over.

Off To A New Beginning

The first day on the Luther campus Tom Johnson studied the bulletin board announcements, items that included the tryout schedule

The Luther Collge Concert Band (c. 1955)
. . . the director did not walk on, he bounced on . . .

for the band, the exact tryout times determined by alphabetical order. All those whose last names ended in J were to show up with their horns at 2 p.m. the next day. Each person trying out would receive a 15-minute audition. No surprises there.

Tom Johnson showed up at his audition with his new Conn trumpet, an expensive graduation gift from grandparents who told him that after all, anybody who would be playing in the Luther College Concert Band deserved a brand new instrument. How he loved that new instrument! How he had practiced! He was prepared; he was confident; he was ready to be put through the paces, and he was, starting with his playing scales, moving onto hitting octaves, sight-reading new music, breath control, triple-tonguing, open and closed tones, vibrato, and amid everything, the person putting Tom Johnson through these paces said essentially nothing. He did not seem impressed either way. When he did talk, he used the imperative case prior to each requirement. The man did say goodbye, however, but even that sounded like an order. But it was all worth it to Tom Johnson. He believed he had performed wonderfully well. Now to reap the reward. Four more years of great trumpeting. After that? Who knows? Certainly a future in music.

The names of those students selected to be in the band were to be posted the following day on a bulletin board located outside the band's practice room. Tom Johnson always liked to see his name on neatly typed lists; it made him feel important. This time it would be especially important. So he went early in the morning to view his important name on the important list. His eyes ran up and down the list of names typed neatly under "Trumpet Section" as he looked for "Tom Johnson." He could not find it. His name did not seem to be there. He looked again; and again. His name did not appear. What happened? Well, there had to be some mistake. This was unnerving, of course, but the situation would easily be corrected by going to see the man in the music department with whom he had his tryout and that man would confirm the error and Tom's name would be added to the important list.

A nervous but still confident Tom Johnson soon found the man in his office and after blurting out his inquiry, the man this time did say a few words, words said deliberately and carefully in only a couple of sentences that settled everything for longer than either would ever know: "Mr. Johnson, I'm sorry to have to tell you that you are not good enough to play in the Luther College Concert Band." The man then began to add something about "practicing more and harder and then maybe next year . . ." but Tom Johnson did not stay to hear any parting words, remembering only the seared-in phrase "You are not good enough . . ." Something happened at that moment, something strange; a response that at the time perhaps made sense only to Tom Johnson. Whatever, Tom Johnson knew right then was that he did not want to play his trumpet ever again. Ever.

It took a couple of hours before Tom's mind cleared enough for him to make a long-distance telephone call. He called the coach at the state college near his hometown to inquire if the basketball scholarship once offered him was still available. It was. "I'll be on your campus tomorrow." He was.

Epilogue

Forty-four years later Tom Johnson would begin his retirement from high school teaching and coaching. By the time of his retirement, he had given up both classroom teaching and coaching and was the school guidance counselor. Forty-four years after walking away from that band-office incident at Luther College, he still had never once touched his new Conn trumpet.

Raising Chickens . . . the Old Fashioned Way

Whaaaat? Talk to a bunch of stupid chickens?

At age 10 her parents decided that she was old enough to take on a special responsibility on their small farm, namely to tend the chickens. Seemed simple enough, easy enough, but it wasn't either one.

The year was 1941. Their farm had no electricity, no furnace, no running water, just an outside hand-pump for water, the tall cast-iron pump with the long, heavy handle, just outside the back door between the wooden clapboard farmhouse and their little summer kitchen.

What this farm had lots of were chickens, some 300 laying Leghorn hens and six roosters. The testosterone-filled roosters easily fulfilled that pleasant task.

However, there was no pleasantness for the 10-year-old who daily dealt with those roosters. They were mean. Constantly she fought off their pecking attacks on her legs, and once when she turned her back, an angry cock flew on top of her back and sunk his gnarly spurs into her flesh until the blood flowed, soaking the whole back of her shirt with blood. She hated those roosters, every one. She was also scared of them. She avoided them whenever possible and took silent, secret delight when any one of them was sent to the chopping block to literally lose their head, which pleasant (for her) ceremony began with the heavy ax blade coming down on their screeching, scrawny necks.

Egg Production

But the hens were different. Not to be feared. And they produced eggs, dozens of eggs every day, with the first picking done in the early morning, the second picking at dusk. Two trips daily to the sagging log henhouse; two trips she came to dislike and at times detest for one reason above any other: the smells. The chicken coop reeked of the pungent, powerful odor of chicken manure. So bad, so strong as to be almost overpowering at times. Sometimes she gagged; sometimes she vomited. Regardless, she went twice daily for these smelly assaults.

The inside of the henhouse was less the charming, cozy chicken coop portrayed in the books of children's fairy tales than it was an indoor, unsanitary ammonia factory. And every spring this heaped, stinking mess on the floor had to be shoveled out

A time period when all farmers had chickens

. . . inside the hen house an unsanitary ammonia factory . . .

the door and tossed on a manure pile. Over the winter months the layers on the dirt floor had built up and up and in the spring, via picks and shovels and manure forks—with grunting and digging and sweating—these layers came down and down and out the door. These work experiences for the 10-year-old produced such a negative sensitivity to those distinctive odors as to never have left her. Never.

Chicken Psychology

To add insult to these experiences, the young girl had to follow "proper procedures" before entering the chicken-coop. First, she had to knock on the door, knock softly and at length. The first time she wrapped on the dilapidated door, with her watchful mother beside her carefully coaching her, she didn't know whether to laugh or cry—or scream! But her mother assured her that the knocking was proper because it gave notice to the chickens inside that someone was coming but they, the chickens, need not worry, what with that proper "introduction" of company.

> *The procedure got worse. She was also ordered to talk to them. "Whaaaaaat? Talk to a bunch of stupid chickens!?"*

The procedure got worse. She was also ordered to talk to them. "Whaaaaaat? Talk to a bunch of stupid chickens!?" "Yup," said the mother, "as you walk in slowly, start talking slowly, softly and steadily. Talk reassuringly so that the chickens will not be frightened and start squawking and flying around and going goofy. A calm voice has a calming effect. You'll see." She saw.

She got more lessons in chicken psychology. "When going to each nest to gather up the eggs, have a quiet conversation with each hen before you reach under her to take her eggs. Then the hen will not resist, not make a fuss, not try to peck you. Makes things easier for both of you." Mom said it; she was right.

Biblical Chickens

But Mom was not right in making her study about chickens, reading those pamphlets brought to their place by the County Agricultural Agent. "Now you just read up 'bout chickens and then you'll 'preciate them more," said the mother. Impossible, thought the daughter. There's force-feeding and now there's force-reading. Whatever, she read and she learned more than she ever cared to know, and learned that nobody knew where chickens ever started in world history, but the guess was that it was somewhere in Southeast Asia a couple of thousand years ago. At the end of every page, she repeated silently to herself, "Who cares?"

Mom cared. Mom believed that chickens were Biblical, stating that even Jesus and the Disciples—and likely Abraham and King David before them—enjoyed gnawing on chicken wings and had hard-boiled eggs for breakfast. This sent the doubting daughter to perusing their well worn family Bible, and there she could not find a single mention of any cock-a-doodle-do in the Old Testament, but she had to concede that the New Testament had the guilt-ridden disciple Peter getting the shameful message upon hearing the cock crowing three times.

The girl did care when she learned that one Leghorn hen could produce 230 to 300 eggs a year. Wow! What really got her head nodding—and nose twitching—was finding out that each laying hen would leave 90 pounds of manure in a lifetime, and that lifetime was only a few years, she told herself that that's one huge pile of poop!

Fall Culling/Cleaning

When the fall season arrived, there was both good news and bad, the good being a large reduction in the flock numbers, culling out dozens of the many older hens that had moved beyond their best egg-laying production. The bad news: all the culled birds had to be butchered.

Butchering was a family affair, an outdoor production task—that found the family doing about a dozen birds a day, the messy, smelly work done in the yard, beside the hand-pump. In the process they used two wash tubs of water, one luke-warm, the other boiling hot, the latter filled with water heated on the kerosene stove inside the summer kitchen, with frequent trips back and forth with the needed hot pails of water for the hot tub.

In an assembly line of three, Pa began by wielding the sharp ax and chopping off the heads—after the wings had stopped their frantic, manic flopping—he plucked out most the outside feathers, after which he handed the half-plucked carcass to Ma who picked off the remaining feathers. This process required the bird to be regularly dunked in and out of the hot water tub as she laboriously picked and pulled out every single embedded follicle. The third person in the process was of course the daughter, charged with digging out the entrails inside the body cavity, making sure to save always the heart, liver and gizzard. Given that 50% of a chicken is edible meat, that requires considerable digging and pulling and dunking. What a mess! What a smell!

The fall butchering added three more offensive odors to the child's overworked nostrils, first the powerful, putrid smell produced by a half-plucked chicken being dunked in and out of boiling hot water, and of course the odors of pulled out entrails, but extra special was the last one, the final singeing of the carcass. For that Ma rolled up a newspaper, lit the end on fire, then picked up the naked bird in one hand and held the burning newspaper to the bird, twisting the carcass around and around to burn off any missed, teensy feather sticking out from the shiny fat skin.

By the end of October the cycle was over for the year, but it would routinely restart in the spring when again the hatchery truck would pull into the farmyard and deliver boxes of tiny chicks, all little peeping, yellow objects so fragile and tiny, all the size of ping-pong balls. Another year, another season, another cycle. This was "the chicken business" as learned and experienced and remembered by a 10-year-old participant "back in the good ol' days." The good old days? They were terrible.

Afterward

Ardis Nieman Noonan described this part of her early life when she was a child living in Olivia, Minnesota. At age 77, when she told this tale, she added that she has tried to forget "that chicken business" but she could not. In later years she said that as an adult she was at first amused by her incurious grandchildren who did not have the slightest understanding of what it was like to raise chickens. She initially found it downright funny when a granddaughter responded to the question of "Where do eggs come from?" with: "They come from the supermarket." Later these kinds of answers became less amusing and really more sad, this lack of even a basic understanding about "the chicken business" the way it once was a way of life for millions of families in rural America.

To the question, Do you still eat chicken? came the answer: "Yes." She also added that when she first breaks the cellophane seal on a package of drumsticks from the supermarket, that certain distinct smell pops out and the memories come flooding back. However, she's glad that the smells of that era are over for her.

TURN ON THE RADIO!
Double Trouble

Ingeborg Tveten was leaving for Church Circle and had to miss the radio broadcast that would be giving a recipe she wanted. So before heading out the door, she directed her husband Lars to listen to the radio and to write down exactly what he heard.

After his wife left, Lars got pencil and paper to do as directed, and to make sure he heard it, he turned on two radios—but each was tuned in to a different station. When the wife got home, she was handed the results of his efforts:

"With hands on your hips, place one cup of flour on your shoulder; raise knees and depress the batter. Mix thoroughly in one-half cup of milk. Repeat this six times.

Inhale quickly one-half teaspoon of baking powder; lower your legs and mash two hard-boiled eggs in a sieve and roll in the whites of two eggs backwards and forward until it comes to a boil.

In 10 minutes remove from oven and rub smartly with a rough towel. After catching your breath, dress in warm flannels and serve with cream of chicken soup. Absolutely delicious."

Shaking Up Community Culture

Tell everybody how good they are?

A spring staple in almost every midwest high school is THE BANQUET, that pleasant gathering of students and parents and grandparents and family members and faculty and school administrators, who get spiffed up to assemble in the school cafeteria for a special dinner.

It's a pleasant pattern. Upon arrival folks socialize a bit nervously and noisily as they indulge in local chitchat before being called in to eat, and after the meal, all settle back to observe the standard rituals that go with the awards ceremony, the reason that brought them all together in the first place. A pleasant gathering indeed.

Of course The Banquet should be plural, there being several school banquets because of the variety of groups and organizations, each wanting its own gathering and not wanting to be all lumped together with others, such as, for example, an All Sports Banquet. No way. There should be separate banquets for each special school group, one just for the wrestlers, for the drama club, the ski club, the honors society, et al.

An attendant staple is the banquet speaker. That person is as much a part of the scripted formula as the audience attitude that the speaker will have the good sense not to be long-winded and never offend anyone with his or her remarks. The speaker should be there just to tell everybody how good they are and what a good school they have.

The Calls

During this banquet season I received a call from a high school principal who asked me to be the speaker at his school's Honor Society Banquet. Fine. However, as to the date there was a problem, said the principal, as he indicated that the exact date would be set only after the basketball squad and the wrestling team had picked their dates.

This scheduling issue should have been the tip-off as to the school's priorities. Still, some schools do not even have an Honor Society, so if the school wants to honor them, go with it. After all, some of us believe that the honors-students are the most important students at a school. Moreover, at any banquet the food is special. As it turned out, the forthcoming "meal" was spe-

Author Art Lee wearing a Norsk *Busserull* . . . *hoping the speaker will not be long-winded* . . .

cial in its own way. Anyway, a few days later a second phone call from the principal indicated the time and date so that all was in order—for the later disorder.

The Gathering

Upon my arrival at the school, groups of students and teachers and town folks were already there, all bubbling and buzzing among themselves, seeing and talking to persons they had not seen for all of two hours. My appearance while walking by, through, and among the assembled could have been that of The Invisible Man. Oh well, plenty of time to walk around and see the whole place, and the long walk was enlightening to observe what was and was not there. My observation came out later in my talk, and though the line was unplanned, just an extemporaneous comment to the effect that "You have a small educational facility surrounded by a large sports complex," or words to that effect.

Meanwhile, back in the cafeteria doorway, the impatient principal stood waiting for what a student told him must have been that stranger wandering around the halls. Our meeting was cordial and perfunctory; for sure it was brief as he immediately hustled me inside and to the empty head table. I sat down and waited. And waited. Finally a student came and sat beside me. I could just as well have remained alone. He did not want to talk. He was the Master of Ceremonies. Maybe he had taken to heart the famous line of President Calvin Coolidge: "I have never been hurt by anything I did not say." He didn't say.

Finally, after some prodding, the young man did allow that he had attended the wrestling-banquet the night before and even half-smiled as he recalled the wonderful chicken dinner that was served and he looked forward even more to the basketball banquet the next week when they would be serving stuffed pork chops. Such food information, so basic and simple and seemingly irrelevant, took on added relevance when we were offered our dinner.

Dinner Time

The head table folks as usual went first through the buffet-style serving line. A beaming, fleshy lady standing at the counter handed each of us a paper plate, a styrofoam cup, and a plastic fork and spoon. So much for banquet silverware. Hence we should not have been surprised when we were served our "meal": a small, square piece of store-bought cherry pie plopped on our paper plates. That was it. The meal. No ice cream to go with the pie; no Cool Whip, no nothing. But we did have a choice of drinks: either warm lemonade or cold coffee. The walk back to the table produced new thoughts, new words, a new speech.

It did not take long for all to finish their pie. Did not take long either for the awards and citations to be handed out to the Honors Students. Didn't take long for the M.C. to introduce the speaker, his entire introduction being: "Well, here's our speaker. He's a history professor." The audience apparently hoped that the speaker (me) didn't take long either. My opening words were meant to be a wry observation on the scene: "Of all the introductions I've had . . . , that was the last one." Nobody laughed.

Ad Lib Time

The title of the talk printed on the program was: "Can You Make It In College?" However, there was no resemblance to the printed title and what was soon stated as my new found topic became 'VALUES,' starting with lots of pointed questions: "What are schools for? Which students should the community most honor? Why? What reveals a town's values? Are these values reflected in its banquets? By the foods served or not served? What students at their banquet deserve to be served pheasant-under-glass? Answer: The Honors Students. Who gets the chicken dinners and the stuffed pork chops? Who should get them? 'Ye shall know the truth, and the truth shall make you . . . change the menu.'"

By this point the superintendent appeared to be looking for a hole to hide in. The principal appeared to be looking for a hole that the speaker might fall in—immediately. A very few parents nodded approvingly; the Honors Students just smiled knowingly. The M.C. day-dreamed through the whole thing.

For the uncomfortable listeners, the best thing about the talk was that it finally ended. The fact that the words hit home was revealed by the applause at the end. It was hardly audible.

Defenestration Time?

A quick exit seemed the pragmatic procedure for the speaker at this point, considering the brief time needed to get the feathers and heat up the tar. I was quickly out-da-dere.

Afterward

Banquet speakers everywhere always wonder if they do any good, if their remarks ever lead to changes in thoughts and actions that are positive. I am proud to report that since my "timely and unprepared remarks" were made that night, that same school has had a Real Banquet Meal—once even stuffed pork chops—every year from then on for its Honors Society members. Yay! Wonderful! And by the way, and not incidentally, I was never invited back again.

There Are Symbols and Then There Are SYMBOLS

A pointed lesson in public reactions to "history"

Author's comment: After teaching school some 40-plus years, there are always a few students and events that one never forgets; this is one of them.)

Eric Torkelson was taking a class in psychology and among his assignments was to do something that would "test public reactions to symbols." He wasn't sure at the start what this was all about, let alone what to do about it, but he and a buddy in the same class got together to talk over possibilities and plans and finally decided on what they originally deemed would be "a great idea." It was great, all right, in that it sure got public reactions!

Eric and friend went to see the head of the Drama Department to inquire about borrowing certain costumes that might be stored in the extensive wardrobe department located in the basement below the college theater. The department head, an older man, listened to their request and then indicated that those costumes—in this case uniforms—were there and they could borrow them but wondered how they planned to use them. After learning of Eric's plan, the man asked: "Are you sure you want to do that? It's not really a good idea. In fact, it's probably risky, even dangerous."

Not the least deterred by this warning, the boys went downstairs and picked out their costumes which in this case were Nazi uniforms, the kind worn by the Nazi Brown Shirts in Hitler's Germany. The uniforms were complete in that they included distinctive Nazi armbands, the ones with the black swastika symbol shown inside a white circle, with a red circle surrounding them, setting off clearly the swastika. The boys also wore the official-looking brown caps and the leather harness around the torso. They even found some black jack-boots, the ones that went all the way to the knees.

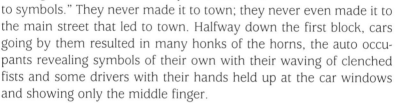

The next morning they put on the full uniforms and the boots and blithely walked off campus, heading for downtown to "test public reactions to symbols." They never made it to town; they never even made it to the main street that led to town. Halfway down the first block, cars going by them resulted in many honks of the horns, the auto occupants revealing symbols of their own with their waving of clenched fists and some drivers with their hands held up at the car windows and showing only the middle finger.

At this point Eric and friend halted, consulted, but bravely kept going to the end of the block, at which point a car pulled up beside them and stopped. The driver, an elderly man, jumped out, put his hands on his hips, and said, "Y'know, boys, I had some dealings with guys like you a few years ago. They called it World War II. Now I'm going down to the Legion club and find a few of my buddies and we'll come right back and talk to you . . ." and he ran back to his car and took off for town.

And Eric and his buddy took off too, but, they took off running back to the campus, back to their dorm rooms where they changed clothes in one big hurry. From this experience—which they never forgot—they truly did learn a pointed lesson about "public reactions to symbols."

(A colleague of mine in the history department taught a course entitled "Modern Germany." The class regularly drew at most a dozen students. Then he decided to change only the title of the same course; he called it "Hitler's Germany." The class filled each time it was offered.)

The month of March in the midwest

Sleds and Sounds and Shocks

"I'm gonna hit the gate!"

There's a standard question asked of older folks, the query that requires pondering. The question: What's your special childhood memory? For most adults, it's seldom just one answer, so the response begins with "Well, it's hard to say, but there was this one time when . . . " and for me it's even harder to say when the answer involves trying to incorporate in the answer a fat dictionary word that is difficult to spell and even more difficult to pronounce. The word is ONOMATOPOEIA (see, I told you so). The definition, however, does make sense: "The formation of a word by imitating the natural sound associated with the action involved." And that makes sense when you come up with words like BUZZ and TINKLE and HISS and RUMBLE and certainly the sound of an old motorboat engine going PUTT-PUTT-PUTT-PUTT. Ah, one can close the eyes and "hear" that boat motor putt-putt-putting along the lake shore.

But what words might catch the sounds made by sled runners gliding smoothly and swiftly over crusted, frozen snow? 'Tis a special, distinctive sound that I can still "hear" in my head; it conjures up a childhood memory of three kids on their Flexible Flyer sleds flying down a long, farm-field hillside, scarves flying out behind, the sleds going so fast that the wind brought tears to the eyes. Oooh how we flew! And our sleds zigged and zagged back and forth across this half-mile stretch of frozen farmland, all the time the sled runners making that distinctive sound as they zipped over the icy land-

scape. It was great; it was magic! A special experience—and with it that unique sound—that made a permanent indentation in the mind, one you can "hear" but cannot put into words. It was something like Tsst-ss-tss-ss-tss . . . Whatever, but whatta day!

The above is the good part. But alas, there's a bad part: the sled-sliding-sounds also bring back the memory of one of those kids ending up that day in a hospital emergency room.

Explanation, Of Sorts

In the Upper Midwest in March, it's a common occurrence in this weird weather month for temperatures to alternate wildly almost daily, sometimes with extreme extremes, like having 70 above one day and the next day it's 20 below zero. During this jumbled weather happening, there can be thick flurries of cold, swirling, pebble-like snow, but strangely within the same HOUR it begins instead to rain. Somewhere in this thermal mess occurs absolutely the greatest sliding conditions ever dreamed of by eager kids.

It had rained much of the previous night on some three feet of snow, the winter's accumulation of white stuff now suddenly soaked. Then it turned cold, real cold, blue-lips, frozen-fingers cold, snow-squeaking-footsteps cold; so cold, said the old men sitting around the hot stove in the blacksmith shop, that the Lutheran pastor's Sunday sermon should be about fire and brimstone, just to heat up the cold church.

For three elementary school kids (my brother and I and the neighbor boy) the cold was not only good, it was perfect! We loved it! Why? Super sliding weather! What's wrong with those old poops who don't like a little cold weather? Haven't they ever gone sliding?

Preparations For The Elements

There's a simple solution for subzero cold: dress for it. Pull on those long-johns; make it two pairs of wool pants, the trouser legs tucked into your 8-buckle overshoes. Get that wool plaid shirt on and pull a bulky wool sweater over that. Now worm your way into your woolen mackinaw, and make sure that woolen stocking cap pulls down

The sliding trio as older high school students: Bob Lee, Bob Bestul, Art Lee
. . . flying down a farm hill . . .

below the ears. Add a double pair of woolen mittens but no leaving the house until your mother has wrapped a wool scarf three times around your neck and face so that only your eyeballs showed. Getting pushed out the door that day were these three, now clothes-fat kids who shuffled forward looking like penguins. We were kind of walking manne-quins advertising for the wool industry. So once outside it seemed appropriate to com-ment: "Jeepers, I sure hope none of us has to pee."

The long walk to the hilltop required entering the field through a farm gate at the bottom of the 10-acre field surrounded by high sheep- fencing. At the entrance gate was barbed wire, six strands of it, stretching from the top of the gate to the top of the snow near the ground. At the start this fence did not seem significant; at the end, well, it would be something else.

The hill we were to walk up was now one huge, tilted skating rink. Pulling a light sled on top of the frozen snow was no problem; keep-ing yourself upright while pulling it, was. Fall down; up again; go a few more steps; fall again, slide back a little; then crawl back up and repeat the shaky, falling, crawling pattern over and over. (Only years later did I believe the Sisyphus Myth to be true.) It sure took a long time to get to the top but finally three now hot and sweating kids made it! We did it! We stood there heroically at the summit! Mount Everest conquered! Hooray!

The view looking back down the long hill was equally good and appreciated all the more for our experiencing the difficulty in get-

ting to that spot. But the wonderment ended, the spell of success broken when the neighbor boy declared out of nowhere: "I don't like that gate down there. I'm afraid I'm gonna hit it." "Whuz-that nonsense? Ahhh, not to worry," we replied; "no problem. Just steer away from it."

Hit The Road—And More

"Enough of this silly talk, C'mon, LET'S GO!" Time to launch properly, that is to be like the Olympic bobsled teams which start with a Run, Run faster, Run and Jump. While adding yells of GERONIMO, we ran and ran and then belly-flopped on top of the sleds, grabbed the wooden steering arms on each side and we were off and soon whooshing downhill at a fast clip that within 25 yards more became a full clip. Flying! Hurtling downward and always that special sound of the sled runners barely touching the surface; TST-SS-TSST-SS. It wasn't a noise as much as it was beautiful singing! Sheer ecstasy! Oooooooo! Fun!

Although there was almost pure ice underneath, the sleds were yet steerable and we would veer left or right and cross over each other's paths and it was all so great, so thrilling until half way down the neighbor boy announced, half hollering: "I'm gonna hit the gate!" It was as though some preordained will had taken him over. We yelled "NOOOooooo, follow us!" And we turned and headed our sleds to the far corner of the field. The neighbor boy kept going straight down the middle of the hill.

His was a seamless slip from denial to fatalism, almost a pronouncement as he screamed the same line one more time: "I'm gonna hit the gate!" He did. Wham! When we finally got to him, he was still entangled in the barbed wire. His abundant outer apparel had protected his body well, but his face was a bloody mess. When he was finally loosed, we headed as fast as we could for the farmhouse, his scarf serving as a big, sopping bandage, but there was still a trail of blood spots behind us in the snow.

Hit The Hospital—But Why?

His mother had seen us coming, seen us running and she knew

something was wrong. Wet wash-cloths came forth quickly but they could not stop the blood flow, the barbs having cut deeply. Then hurried talk between the parents before the decision. Then into the car they ran for a fast trip to the Doctor, but as it turned out, the damage was minimal. A few stitches in the upper lip, a couple of stitches more on cuts above the eyes and along the hairline, and that was all. No damage done to the eyes; no torn nose; no ripped off ears. He lucked out, considering the force with which his sled hurtled into the bending but unyielding barbed wire gate.

Later came the obvious question to him: why did he do it? Why this fixation when he could easily have steered away from the gate? He said he didn't know; he could not explain it, saying only that he just couldn't force himself to turn away. He didn't know why. Neither did we. (Still don't.)

Meanwhile, the sliding conditions were so great that day that my brother and I planned to go the next day, too. Alas, not to be. The fickle weather had suddenly turned warm; the thaw came that night so no more hard snow; the sled runners would sink in. It was over. But the mysterious sounds of the sled runners on hard crusted snow still remain; I can hear them now . . . Tsst-ss-tss-ss . . .

(Long) Afterward

The injured boy that day was named Robert Bestul; he grew up to become a high school band director in several Wisconsin towns, finishing his career and retiring in Viroqua, Wisconsin. He passed away from Alzheimer's in 2007 at age 77. My brother Bob—Robert E. Lee—also became a band director, retiring from Wartburg College after 35 years there; he still lives in Waverly, Iowa. We both remember that sliding-event as though it were, well, only yesterday . . .

Facts You've Likely Never Thought About or Even Wanted to Know

Of the over six billion people in the world, their total numbers/percentages are represented by the number 100.

60 Asians	51 male
14 Africans	49 female
12 Europeans	
8 Latin Americans	67 non-Christian
5 U.S. & Canada	33 Christian
89 heterosexual	82 non-white
11 homosexual	18 white

5 control 33% of the wealth and all 5 are from the U.S.

80 live in substandard housing

7 cannot read

1 has a college education

Mirror, mirror on the wall, where's
the bestest food of all?

Where There's Real
Food and Lots of It!

Eating Out—The American Way

"Eating Out" is so common and so popular nowadays that at least
once a year the thick, slick magazine MINNESOTA MONTHLY
devotes an entire issue to just this subject, with a recent issue sprin-
kling small headlines on the cover, like "GOURMET GETAWAYS,"
"57 Restaurants Worth The Drive." The mag offers even a play on
words: "We Meat Again: Fogo De Chao's Steak On A Sword."
Ahhhh, the promotion of food, Food, FOOD!

Moreover, each just-plain regular issue of MINNESOTA MONTHLY
devotes its last section to "DINING GUIDE," listing page after page
of restaurants and pubs and cafes and buffets and bars and grills
and delis, all presumably hot spots where the finest cuisine available can be found for those with deep hunger—and deep pockets.
All this special food for the special Twin Cities natives.

(Some readers of the MONTHLY could easily conclude that upon driving out of the cities, if you cannot see the IDS tower on the skyline in
the rearview mirror, it's all downhill for dining after that, the food's
unpalatable outside the city limits. Good food only in the metro area?
One might think that the only thing left to eat north of Coon Rapids
is chopped liver and smelly onions, south of Burnsville half-cooked
pancakes and oily bacon; east of Woodbury tuna casserole with tater-
tots on top, west of Chanhassen scrambled eggs and spinach, soggy
toast and weak cold coffee, all this slop for just 10 bucks.)

Keep On Going

But the Twin Cities natives should move out, way out; get beyond the suburbs, get out into the small towns and mingle with the country folks because "out there" they'll find real comfort in real comfort foods, always in the local church dinners and suppers. Now that's good eating! And so inexpensive! There's nothing to match a great CHURCH SUPPER!

There's a rule-of-thumb, that seems to hold true: the smaller the town, the more remote the church, the smaller the congregation, the better the food—and there's more of it.

Case In Point #1

Leonard, Minnesota (it's a little difficult to locate, all right, but it is there, somewhere in The Great Northwest); town's population, 29; church membership, 49 families (currently served by an 88-year-old retired Lutheran pastor). Each Fall the Leonard Lutheran Church—Our Savior's—holds a Meatball Dinner, starting at 3 in the afternoon and lasting until 7 p.m., or until the last patron is served, whatever. At the end they will have served over 600 meals. The food is served in the basement; there's no pretense, no euphemisms, no "Fellowship Hall" designation. It's simply a basement with iron round pillars to hold the place up and dodge with your plate; a downstairs with gray tile flooring and kids' Sunday School pictures on the walls amid rosemaled plates hanging there year-round and a big line of cut-out letters by the front serving table reading "Come Lord Jesus . . . Be Our Guest . . . " And there's rows of long tables with squeaky metal folding-chairs on each side, just waiting for customers; and then there's the food.

The Real Food—meat and potatoes—are first served buffet style by robust ladies (the men are back in the kitchen scrubbing pots and pans and mashing the vats of potatoes—real potatoes! Not the phony kind, not those "instant potatoes" you get in some restaurants). Anyway, one starts the eating-orgy by walking to the serving line, picking up a big plate, then receiving all the mashed potatoes desired; being awarded as many meatballs and all the great brown gravy desired; then you take a spoonful of diced carrots and head for your table, there to find much more: help yourself to pickled beets and tasty sweet-and-sour pickles and cranberries; and a big dish of coleslaw, a dish of rice-pudding, a basket of hot home-made rolls; plates with sticks of real butter, and a BIG plate of home-made lefse slices (and a bowl of sugar for the finicky) and flatbrød (flat bread). Help yourself to all that's there! Fill up your plate at least twice. If you don't take seconds, it's assumed you've had your stomach stapled.

When finally finished eating all that food on the big plate—and this takes a long while—then comes the little plate with the homemade pie offerings, the selection of the little plate being difficult because of the variety offered and each big piece looks so good. Wash all the above down with coffee, real coffee, black and hot and strong; it ain't just tan, luke-warm water in those church coffee mugs. By this time, of course, en full mage (a full stomach). Uff da. Time to stop. Time to push yourself up and waddle out the door and make room for those hungry folks still sitting and squirming upstairs in the church sanctuary waiting for their seating numbers to be called so they too can hustle down and receive COMFORT. And the cost for this eating-orgy? $6.00.

Move On To Lutefisk

For the uninitiated folks who wonder about that word lutefisk: lute (means lye); fisk (means fish); lutefisk is a cod, the skinned fish initially soaked in a special lye-solution, then soaked/cleansed in ice-cold water before finally being "ready" to be boiled "just right" before serving. If the preparation of the cod is just right, a platter of hot lutefisk will lie on the serving table and just jiggle and wiggle without anyone having jiggled or wiggled the table. It's alive!(?) What ingredients go on the fish? Depending, Swedes

> *If the preparation of the cod is just right, a platter of hot lutefisk will lie on the serving table and just jiggle and wiggle without anyone having jiggled or wiggled the table. It's alive!(?)*

prefer a cream-sauce poured over the cod while Norwegians like melted butter on it. As to The Basics that go with any lutefisk supper anywhere, all Scandinavians like lefse (much preferred over bread or rolls) and both ethnic groups like boiled potatoes and both like mashed rutabagas along with coleslaw.

Added condiments vary widely, including the extreme one lute-fisk-lover who brings with him to every supper a bottle of Tabasco sauce. There seems to be no middle ground on eating lutefisk; one either loves it or hates it (the latter eat the meatballs). And the jokes about lutefisk are never ending, even including theological applications, e.g. "It's the Cod that passeth all understanding"; or "In Cod we trust."

Desserts following the main meal again vary, again depending on how pure Scandinavian the cooks are (ambition fits in this formula, too). If ekte Norsk (strictly Norwegian), there'll be rømmegrøt or kringle or rosettes. Otherwise pies or strudel.

Case In Point #2

AARDAHL, Minnesota. Population: 0 (there is no town; it's in Beltrami County); there is no nothing in Aardahl; it's just a little white wooden-framed church out in the country, standing at a quiet four-corners, the ELCA congregation first organized in 1896 (unless you know where to find it, you can't get there from where you are). Aardahl church membership: 70 families (currently served by the Rev. Arlen Stensland who serves both Aardahl and Malvik, the latter little church also serving succulent walleye and roast pork suppers). The Aardahl church members have been serving lutefisk suppers there since the 1930s so the folks around Aardahl have had a long time to figure out the whole process, starting with making sure there's sufficient quantities of the fish. For their recent supper (2007), they ordered 400 pounds of lutefisk and in serving 463 meals that night, that's a lot of lutefisk per person, uff da.

As to its fame? And how does it rate? Compare? Well, the rule-of-thumb as applied to the quality of the meals served in the region has reached the point where the proper summary-line reads: "There

are lutefisk suppers served everywhere, y'know, and THEN THERE IS THE AARDAHL LUTEFISK SUPPER!" It's in a class by itself. Or as one aficionado phrased it, the burly man, a true descendent of the Great Snoose Chewers of the Viking Age: "It don't get no better den Aardahl." Another partisan patron, who leaves every fall to spend the winters in Texas, will never leave home and become a snowbird until after he has had his annual lutefisk-fix at Aardahl!

The church is small; the eating area off to the side is smaller (they moved up from the basement five years ago). Officially the serving begins at 4:30, which means they start eating by 4:00, which means that a crowd is there by 3:00, which means the bulk of the hungry horde better

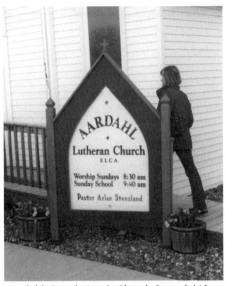

Aardahl; Population 0; Church Served 463 Suppers

. . . "out there" in rural america folks will find real comfort food . . .

get there by 5:00 and then they will likely still have to wait two hours or more before being called to dine. Ahh, but it's worth the wait.

CASES #3, #4, and more . . . will have to wait; they're good, too; they're all good but it's just that some are "gooder" than others.

More Than Food

Church Suppers are about more than just about food. They fulfill many needs, desires, and goals. They're great social events, a great place to meet old friends and to meet new ones (some of the latter turn out surprisingly to be members of their same congregation). For the work and workers required—there's a common spirit of friendship and cooperation; a semi-family-togetherness, a congregational unity, if only for a day or two. It's rewarding for church leaders to see so many of their parishioners together in a common cause, and these same leaders wish that that unity would carry over the entire year. And not to be overlooked, for tiny churches, their annual church supper is A, if not, THE major factor in meeting their financial budget-goals for the year. Church suppers are work and fun and good, and they're important for all kinds of good reasons.

Spread The Word?

If only those Twin Cities folks could know what they're missing. The poor things. Maybe we should tell them; sort of spread the word about where to go to find great meatballs and lutefisk suppers. But nei/no. Let's not, because on second thought, it's just as well they don't know as the waiting lines to eat at Leonard and Aardahl and all the other churches are long enough the way they are. Jo da, "Let them eat cake."

Henrik Odegaard went to the doctor's office and said to the doctor: "Ya, den, Doc, my wife she t'inks she'ss a schicken! Do yew 't'ink yew kin cure her, den?"

Doctor: "Yes, Henrik, I believe that I can cure your wife of her belief that's she's a chicken."

Henrik: "Ya da, but I'm not so sure dat I vant her cured."

Doctor: "Huh? Why not?"

Henrik: "Yew see, da problem iss ve need da eggs."

Are We Heinz 57 Citizens?

Globilization. Outsourcing. The Internet. World-Connecting-Cell-Phones. iPods. Blackberrys. Whew! They're all there. The Information-Age has descended with electronic thuds. All the above have changed the way Americans try to understand themselves and our cultural and ethnic identities.

We no longer are strongly bound with just American culture, let alone a specific ethnic heritage. That Big World out there is no longer out there; it's here! And we face uncertain times.

"Made In Japan"—Ha Ha

Confusing times, especially for the ethnic-interested. For example, how can Scandinavian-Americans, or any other ethnic grouping, maintain an identity in a country with already many cultures—now invading our once-little world? Years ago "Made in Japan" suggested shoddy products, so bad that the phrase used to be a joke. No more. Now it suggests quality.

Only a couple of generations ago we were surrounded primarily by people we knew personally and trusted and with whom we bonded. Our own group; our own people; our own proper-way-of-living, or so we pronounced it to be. Once we were insulated; semi-isolated. No more. New times. New pressures. New products. New cars—and hardly just Fords, Chevys, and Chryslers; nowadays they're likely "Made In Japan." And no one laughs, least of all General Motors.

The "Me" Groupings

We have been thrust into becoming global citizens. The problem of heritage-maintenance applies to all ethnic groups just trying to hang on to their heritage. It ain't easy.

An admitted problem, of course, that critics seldom fail to mention: is that tribal identities (e.g. think solid/stolid Norwegians) tend to create stubborn boundaries around themselves that often lead to resistance if not hostilities towards other groups, sometimes including other Scandinavians. It's hard to get much accomplished that's positive within a narrow minded and limited loop of "the tribe." For some, it's still "them versus us. Everyone is wrong except you and me, and I'm not so sure about you." Ignorance is selfish bliss.

However, on the other hand, a current absence of any ethnic identity (think "Heinz 57 citizens") leads to no social bonding at all, which makes it difficult to address even local concerns. It's hard to get together. Hence, let "them"—"the government"—do it, not us. Social insulation/isolation. Who knows their neighbors any more? Who cares to know them? Leave me alone. What's the center of the universe? Me, of course. It is curious but true that one of the few things that will bring neighbors together is a neighborhood tragedy; a "good house fire" can actually be socially beneficial, alas.

The Good That Can Come Out . . .

Is this globalism good or bad? Or neither?

Obviously, globalism has helped make ethnic heritage less important, less relevant, less interesting. This can be confirmed by membership chairmen of ethnic organizations everywhere trying to sign up new and younger members. On the plus side, globalism makes all citizens more informed if not enlightened. It's both modern and useful to think as world citizens and move freely among different cultures while appreciating something in all of them. One doesn't have to be fat to be well-rounded.

And not incidentally, the Global Citizen can easily proclaim the line: "Hey, I can be Scandinavian too." Anyone can learn about

Scandinavian culture and "become one of them"—well, at least for a little while, at least until the churches' lutefisk and torsk and meatball suppers are over for the Fall season.

For all ethnic groups "hanging on," maintaining their heritage, there's the ongoing need for these societies to highlight their heritage. Reach out; lighten up; rethink those stereotypes. Who knows but all this Globalism might start with Norwegian-Americans admitting: "Yeah, maybe dose Svedes ain't such bad fellers after all, den."

Crudeness? Ignorance?
Whatever, the Deal Was Made

There is a metal file made by a company called Bastard. Not knowing this fact can lead to some curious misunderstandings, as described below. Not incidentally, that event became one of the favorite stories told and retold by the hardware store owner.

Siri Blekken walked into the hardware store, sent there by her husband to buy a file, a product with which she was vaguely familiar. The store owner, Johan Hanssen, took her over to look at the several varieties of files available. Johan began by grabbing a big file, holding it up to show her, and stating: "This big Bastard costs the most but it's worth it, then."

Mrs. Blekken looked over the big fat file, and as she pondered the purchase price, Mr. Hanssen picked up another file, not quite as big, and said: "Well, here's kinda a medium-sized Bastard that should work just fine, but it costs almost as much as that big Bastard."

Again Mrs. Blekken thought about it but didn't want to pay that much either, and so she picked up the smallest file lying there and then asked: "Well, then, how much is this little S.O.B.?" Hanssen had to restrain himself from laughing before telling her the price and the price was just right for Mrs. Blekken.

Now a satisfied customer, out the door she went with the little Bastard, leaving behind a bemused store owner who could hardly wait to begin relaying the story.

Time to Let Students Make Their Contribution

AN EXPLANATION of sorts for the following section as it obviously does not fit into any book that is essentially about SCANDINAVIANS IN AMERICA, even if the subjects—i.e. former students of mine—were either in or from Scandinavian-dominated communities, however, what students wrote for their test-answers makes for interesting—reading. These answers may make some readers laugh, others cry; these student observations are worth passing on.

Setting The Stage

Nationally acclaimed television comedians hire the best and brightest joke-writers. Situation-comedy programming requires script writers with proven successes behind them. Humor-columnists search diligently to discover the best anecdotes and quips. But none of these writers could conjure the innovative "gags" that come from the pencils and pens of public school students as they plow (fake?) their way through examinations.

The Quality Of Mercy

Who but a student would admit: "I have advanced from an economic illiterate to an economic dim-wit." Who but a pensive pupil would offer in the same "answer" three versions of the definition of HEGEMONY: "It means having more than one wife. Then again 'heg' means eight, so it must be an eight-sided marriage. Ah, heck, I'll bet it's what a guy yells when he finds a diamond lying in he street and turns it in to a jooler (sic) and says, 'Hey! Gem! Money!'"

Consider the imagery demonstrated in this description: "A bicycle pulled up and two women jumped out." And what seems more common-sensical than the reasoning behind this student's explanation of the SUBMERGED LAND ACT: "It was an act which gave farmers money to plow up land under water." How about the WORKS PROGRESS ADMINISTRATION? (the WPA) "It was an congressional act in the Depression years to help men relieve themselves." And more strained logic in the definition of the big word for a nose bleed, EPISTAXIS: "It's a Mexican word for a cab driver. Either that or a new form of income tax."

'TIS TIME TO GO CHRONOLOGICALLY through early American History as perceived—at least on exam paper—by some of my public school students who at that time of their writing ranged from 9th to the 12th grade. All items below are actual students answers! No one could make these answers up.

America's Early Years

"Norsemen call the Indians 'skrellings" which means they were war-whoppers."

"The Puritans started schools soon after their arrival so that their children would not be led into evil by Satin."

"None in our family were descendants of immigrants. We were always just here. Oh, by the way, there is a joke in our family that we belong to the Venetian Blind Irish."

Question: How authentic is Minnesota's Kensington Rune Stone? Answer: "It is very authentic because no one really knew much about him. He was really a great guy."

Colonial Times

"The Indians sold Manhattan Island to the Dutch for a poultry 24 dollars."

"Before the Franch and Indian War began, the Franchmen began moving south from Canada, and the Virgins, sensing danger, began to build a fort."

American Revolution

"Someone in England said Boston should be punished for the Tea Party and destroyed like ancient Cartridge."

"The missteake in the picture showing Washington crossing the Delaware is that it was the Hudson he crossed."

"The book on Benedict Arnold was slanted in such a way as to not make him a trader but a hero."

Author at the podium (professor for 35 Years)
. . . *his history of BSU 541 pages long (ouch!); good doorstop* . . .

The Federalist Period

"Washington's Farewell Address is much adieu about nothing. It was boring."

"Washington annointed John Adams as his vice president."

"The Federalist Papers were written by Huntley and Brinkley."

"Washington, D.C. became our capital as soon as Hamilton and Jefferson rolled some logs out of the way."

The Constitution

"The system of our checks and balances works very simply. Before you can write any checks, you must have a balance."

"When John Adams was President, Congress passed the Alien and Sedation Acts."

"John Adams was called 'His Rotundity' because he was the original 'Mister Five By Five.'"

Jeffersonian Era

"He got out of jail on a horpus-corpus."

"He obtained his release on a Writ of Corpus Christy."

"If Jefferson were alive today and could see what his party is doing, he would turn over in his grave."

Question: What official administers the oath of office to the new U.S. President? Answer: "The Pope."

Teacher's assignment: Read any article in NEWSWEEK; then write down and hand in any new words that you found. Next day came the answer to new words: "tantalize, ideology, intransigent, goddammit."

Promotion Time; Let The College Freshmen Take Over

Author's intrusion (again). After nine years of teaching in junior and senior high school—and these were in retrospect wonderful years with great kids—this author began teaching in a college. Fear preceded this change as I anticipated major differences in the intellectual abilities of college students that might overwhelm me. Turned out there was little to fear as there was/is little difference between 12th graders and "13th graders," that is, college freshmen. (Yet one difference did stand out: when high school kids are bored, they act up; when college students are bored, they go to sleep.)

A proper perspective: The bizarre student answers below represent only those "special few." It is thus unfair to the great majority of students whose answers were good and solid—but not half as interesting. There is a valid comparison to be made with newspapers. They print what is interesting and new, The News. Their basic position is summed up in the standard lines: "Dog bites man." That's not news, but "Man bites dog" is news. So too with student-exam-answers; it's the goofy ones that stand out, e.g. "Senator Robert LaFollette was hanged in Effigy, Wisconsin."

Definitions

Red Herring: A good eating fish.

Yellow Press: This refers to the discrimination against the Chinese who were pressed into working in laundries.

Free and Unlimited: The gold was running short and the government started issuing worthless paper Coinage of Silver which wasn't worth anything so the gold became priceless. It was around the Depression Age. Really, I don't know what the hell it's all about.

Autonomy: The study of autos.

French Salons: A place where nasty men went to drink beer.

The Mann Act: An act for women to improve American morale.

Rebate: When a resolution doesn't pass the first time, the senators bring it up again for a rebate.

Rebate: Well, when the worm falls off the hook, it's time to rebate it.

Anachronism: The guy who shot President McKinley was an anachronist.

Life-Space-Area: That period in life in which one looks into space for the right answers.

Philology: The science of love, phil meaning love and ology meaning science.

Jesuits: The founder of the Society of Jesus, the Jesuits, was Martin Luther.

Correspondence With Students

Question to the Professor: "Is it correct that term papers for you require an animated bibliography.?

Letter from a student sent to the Records and Personnel Office:

"Dear Personal:

"I have recieved my grades yesterday and found a mistack. I feel I should have goten a A for my freshman english course. I do not know wether Prof. _____ will be working this summer so can see my final's test. Please corect my First-Aid grade too and send the enclosed letter through intercollege mail."

Lines Taken From Essay Exams

"Sen. Eugene McCarthy had a kind heart and a good mind but that's no good in running for President" . . . "Pres. Kennedy was said to be full of whit and vigger." . . . "With his references to fat japs and stupid pollacks, vice president Spiro Agnew castarated himself" . . . "The Mann act was not about man. They didn't want hores going from one state to another" . . . "Thorstein Veblen lived during the time of the Big Typhoons" . . . "Eugene Debs was our President at the turn of the censury" . . . "People lived in poor homes and had little money. In summary, these people were living in puberty" . . . "Erasmus, a monk, left the monkery at the age of 22."

"After Elizabeth succeeded to the thrown, people of England felt unsure and a sense of unrest ran through their mines" . . . "In fact, the King had such an insignificant role that even I have forgotten his name" . . . "In England approxamately 10% were nobility; 94% of the country were pheasants" . . . "Libel means its bound to happen, like a guy is libel to get hurt" . . . "Plutocracy is the time or situation described by Pluto."

"June 6, 1944, is officially known in America as V-D Day" . . . "Hugo Black was a Supreme Court member and also a KKK member. This presented a confliction" . . . "This huge bird flew over my canoe; I had never seen a Great Blue Herring before" . . . "Anarchy means the rule of one person as represented by our President" . . . "After Gen. MacArthur got canned in Korea, he wrote a famous song called

'Old Soldiers Never Die, They Just Fade Away'" . . . "The Gross National Product is a special plant grown only in the USA" . . . "The U.S. state department was filtered by Communists" . . . "In Natural Selection, the fit will survive over the week" . . . "The Wabash Court Case declared the constitution unconstitutional."

(So many of the unintentional errors came from spelling problems and are "harmless." However, on occasion a wrong letter results in a major shock, as illustrated by the student asked to identify Cyrus McCormick. He wrote that "Cyrus McCormick did a wonderful thing; he invented the reaper." However, in his spelling of the last word, he omitted the first letter "e." He then added: "It did the work of a thousand men.")

Indentification

Eva Braun: She was the first lady U.S. Congressman.

W.E.B. DuBois: In the 1920s he headed the Ku Klux Klan.

Joseph Pulitzer: He invented dynamite to keep the peace.

A. Mitchell Palmer: He headed the Palmer Raids, which were panty raids.

Henry Wallace: He was the Grand Master of the KKK who attacked his secretary in a hotel and she died of bitewounds. Now that's what I call a dirty old man.

Admiral A.T. Mahan: He was a firm believer in navel strategy.

Karl Marx: He wanted to start something in which people get things without money. A good example of this today is potluck.

Attila: The first pope to be chosen head of the church.

Jane Adams: She started Hull House. This was a place for bartered women.

Tom Watson: An unknown American Populist doctor until he went to England and joined up with Sherlock Holmes.

Trygve Lie: With a name like that, he had to be a chinaman.

Ezra Taft Benson: Second female to be in a U.S. Cabinet. She was also black, I think. Then again maybe not.

Dr. Klaus Fuchs: Despite his obscene name, he fled the U.S. to avoid the hassles of the Commie haters.

And lastly, a response to the question: "Name three Native American Indian Tribes."

ANSWER: "The Nina, the Pinta, and the Santa Maria."

Family Names in America

Where they come from and what they mean

There are a few of us—likely VERY few—who are interested in Norwegian-American family names as to their origin and what they mean in Norwegian (if anything; some are simply not to be translated). Family names is an interesting project, we believe, but lots of caveats show up before even starting to explore this subject.

It's a complicated business, full of exceptions and eccentricities and changes in orthography (pertains to correct spellings) over the centuries, both in Norway AND America, the latter location because upon arriving and settling in the U.S., immigrants often changed or modified their old country names and took what they often called their "Amerika-navn" (American names) more suited to their new home.

Anyway, let's start with the family SURNAME, which the dictionary translates as "in modern times, the last or family name shared by all members of the same family." In 19th century Norway, the century of migration, there was by then a semi-standard formula in the naming of a new baby, which included giving the infant three names only: a first name, a middle name, and last/surname. While the first name would be different (there was once a fuzzy formula for first- name selections too but that's really complicated), the middle name would USUALLY be the father's first name followed by SON if a boy or DATTER if a girl, and then the last name which would usually be taken from the name of the gård (farm) or the place where the family had lived. (Norway's population in the 19th century was by far the most rural of all the Scandinavian countries.)

Farm names in Norway have stayed the same for centuries and are subsequently listed in their current official regional-record-books (bygdeboker), which books inform the reader of the names of the families who have lived on such-and-such a farm over several centuries. Obviously these books are valuable for Americans trying to trace their ancestry in Norway. However, to make genealogy efforts more difficult—and this comes as a surprise to some readers—a Norwegian family who moved from

Thus if that same family moved several times, each time there would be a different last name for this same family.

one farm to a different farm would regularly take the name of their new farm for their last name. Thus if that same family moved several times, each time there would be a different last name for this same family. (Also factored in is the fact that Norway was under Danish rule for some 400 years, hence the influence Danish spellings "of Norwegian names"; this is true up to the present time.)

Illustrations (Hoping They're Helpful)

To try to explain and illustrate the above paragraph, I'll use my own emigrant grandfather whose name in America was LARS AGRIMSON LEE (1856-1943). Lee is spelled Li in Norwegian; Lie in Danish.) Lars' father was named Agrim Jacobson Li—although his last name had previously been Breistøl but because his family had moved to the Li farm, their last name then became Li. Grandfather Lars had seven siblings (there were two girls and six boys) and all eight had "Agrimson/datter" for their middle name; six came to America, two stayed in Norway.

All the Lee family emigrants who came to the U.S. agreed to keep the same last name but Americanize the spelling to Lee, but this was not always done by many families. While most immigrants kept the old family name, others changed it in the U.S., with spelling changes being the most common. But some went for entire changes, perhaps a name for the valley (dal) from which they came or perhaps to some geographic site back in the old country, like Foss (waterfall). To make it even more difficult for some present-day Americans to trace their family history, some immigrants from the same family ALL chose different last names when they arrived to begin life in the new world.

Translations

Whatever the family name immigrants used in America, almost all those names can be "translated" at least in part from what they mean in Norwegian. Again to illustrate, I'll start with the name Lee (Li in Norsk) which means simply hillside. (P.S. Ben Franklin was right in noting that he would not talk about himself so much if he only knew anyone else half as well.) Consider the common spin-offs of that Lee/Li/Lie name in America (also add spelling changes) and you come up with: Nordlie (the north side of the hill), Westley (west side), Sorlie (south side), Bratlie (steep side), and more variations beyond those mentioned.

Consider families in the U.S. with "Skog" (means woods/forest) somewhere in their last name, e.g. Skogerboe (farmstead in a woods), Skoglund (forested grove), Skogfjord (woods on water), Nyskogen (new forest). And the many name-spinoffs from "Mo" (means meadow or flat land): Moen (the field), Gardemoen (farm/military field), Moebakken (field with hill), and on and on.

Geography And Names

From olden times, even going back before the birth of Christ, families in Norway have had their names based on the places where they lived, the aforementioned Gård (farm) or Grend (farm groupings), Fjell (mountain) or Aaser (forested ridges), Elver (rivers) or Fjords or Vik (bay/inlet) or Øyer (islands) or Holmer (rock islands). How many location-places and hence family-names? Researchers suggest there were more than a million such "place names," and many of course also ended up in the U.S. as family surnames, e.g. Buksengaard (the goat farm). Note the double-A used in America

to get the same sound of that odd Norwegian letter "a" with the little loop over it: å; the sound is close to "oh" and "au."

Looking at a Norwegian map helps in giving the background of some names that are still in America, and there are lots of them: Storvik (big bay), Borge (castle/fort), Bree (glacier), Fjellstad (mountain place), Haugen (the hill), Seter (mountain farm; in the U.S. often changed to Sather or Sether or Sathre); Holten (the grove), Hove (worship site of old gods), Engen (the pasture), Nes (usually spelled Ness in U.S.; means penninsula); Havstad (harbor place); Elvestad (river place), Strand (beach), and Sund (strait). The latter two are often combined with another location, e.g. Strandjord (beach/ground) and Sundvold (sunny, grassy plain).

Especially farm-names (gård is a farm) can tell much about the olden days, including the Viking age (800-1050), as many were combined with ancient gods, such as Thorgård and Frigård, and with Christianity came appropriate farm names too, e.g. Prestgård (the priest/pastor's farm) or Kirkegård (the church farm) as well as appropriate Christian first names: Mathias, Markus, Lukas, Pål, Johannes, Peder, Andreas, Maria, Margareta, Katarina, Anders, Margit, Karen, and Kari—and lots more.

The Hanseatic (German controlled shipping) League in Norway in the middle ages added German influence in some names/spellings, e.g. Henrik, Herman, and Gjertrud.

As stated, the Danish domination of Norway for four centuries (until 1814) caused the Norwegian spelling of SON to sometimes be changed to the more Danish SEN, hence Andersen, Nilsen, Jensen, Hansen, and Pedersen. They're still Norwegians.

Even More Background: Aspects And Factors In Names

The great share of gård/farm and stad/place-names (e.g. Fredrikstad, Grimstad) in Norway were determined between 1000 and 2000 years ago. However, some names are more recent as new lands were cleared for farming—often marginal farming—due to population growth in the 17th and 18th centuries. Also in these latter centuries some old gaard/farm names were subdivided with new prefixes, and thus the original Tun (site of a dwelling with courtyard) might be added Øvre (east) tun, Mid (middle) tun, Nedre (lower) tun, and other variations. (In the U.S. it's "Thune.")

Then came the Age of Reason and with it the drive for centralized efficiency and record-keeping in governments, including that of Denmark-Norway. (Norway did not get its own constitution until 1814, and not full independence until 1905.) Starting with military conscripts and then expanding to all male adults in the kingdom, all were required to register a permanent family surname with the state in the latter 18th century. Most chose the name of their home gaard (note American spelling for gård), if they owned one, or if cotters/husmenn ("renters") the farm-name on which they were contractually bound.

Those without ties to a home farm might choose a place- name in their home region (e.g. Storsund) or their patronymic (father's name) as their permanent surname and that of their descendants, therefore likely the prevalence still of Olsons, Larsons, Swensons, Kristoffersons, et al. in today's modern Norway.

Of major importance was The Great Emigration (out-migration) of the 19th and early 20th centuries to America (800,000-plus left—almost 30% of the Norwegian population). With their immigration (in-migration) came the opportunity to "rename" themselves—or be renamed by some immigration official at the port of arrival where registration was required (immigration centers like Castle Garden in New York city until 1892; at Ellis Island after that). Although there were a host of strange if not goofy personal choices, there was yet

a common pattern followed by most Norwegians:

1) Keep the family gaard/farm name intact as a surname (e.g. Henningsgaard) and/or modify its spelling and/or reduce the syllables to conform to English better, making it both easier to spell and pronounce by American speakers, e.g. Ruspesteensgaarden became just plain Steen, and Karl Nilssen became Carl Nelson in America.

2) Attempt some English translation of the old gaard name or home region, e.g. Øksvig (ox-bay) became Axvig; Myrfjeld (marshy mountain farm) became Mayfield; Gustavus Bestøl (an out-farm) became Gus Bestul; Gunholt Greinegaard became Glen Green.

3) Go patronymic. Abandon the farm or place names entirely and opt for the simple and pronounceable first name of the male head of the family as their permanent last name in America, hence the great numbers of descendents today with SON or SEN endings. To illustrate their numbers, go to the Minneapolis telephone book and look up the name JOHNSON; then, after all those pages, go to the JOHNSENS; next the JOHANSONS AND JOHANSENS; on to the JOHANNESSONS et al. variations—but you get the idea.

Winding Up (this mess)

More Norsk-word-parts, their different spellings, what they mean, and finally that part of the word found in American names:

- våg, vaag = meaning bay, and found in America by persons like Ole Rølvaag (means noisy, unruly bay)

- by, bo, boe, bø = from Old Norse for farmstead, place of residence; later applied to a village or town which grew on this site; found in names like Dorothy Boe, Arvid Midbo, Don Bye

- rud, rude, rød, rødde = Old Norse for cleared-land; Americans like Ole Evinrude, Clara Colrud, Gordon Trinrud

- eid, eide = an isthmus of land; marshy-isthmus farm; seen in the U.S. in names like Eric Severeid

- svee, sveum, sveen = a farm cleared by burning; names like Paul Sveum

- tveit, tvedt (Danish), tveiten = cleared land; in U.S. as in Solveig Tveit; often spelled Tweet; or as in Jerry Tweeten

- stad, sted = place of residence in Old Norse; later a village, town, city; as in Phil Hofstad, Loren Hemsted

- stu, stue, stuggu = family dwelling, main house, room; as in Mildred Skogstu, Sigurd Krostue, Joe Haugstugge

- vang, vangen = grassy plain; seen in names like Arve Wang, Camilla Wangen

- voll, vold (Danish), vollen = rolling plains; names like Koren Hjemvoll, Herman Vollen, Viola Vold

Factoids

- Ole, of "Ole Olson" fame: the name Ole is actually a Danish form of the Norwegian Olav.

- Some of the most common names in Norway originate from Christianity. Both Hans and John are short forms of Johannes. Some others are Kristian, Kristen, Christian, and Christoffer/Kristoffer. (When searching the 1865 census database for names starting with "Christ," there are 30 variations listed.)

- The introduction of double-names started in the 1800s resulting, for example, in a family of four boys being named Johan-Bendic, Johan-David, Johan-Leif, Johan-Lars.

No wonder (from the above—all of it—) genealogy searches can be so difficult for Americans trying to figure out their ancestry. That said, it's still fun! It is! It's rewarding detective work.

I Am Thankful For . . .

☐ the mess to clean up after a holiday because it means I have been surrounded by family and friends

☐ the taxes I pay because it means that I have income

☐ the clothes that fit a little too snug because it means I have enough to eat

☐ my shadow who watches me work because it means I am out in the sunshine

☐ a lawn that needs mowing, windows that need washing, and gutters that need fixing because it means I have a home

☐ the spot I find at the far end of the parking lot because it means I am capable of walking

☐ my large heating bill because it means I am warm

☐ the lady behind me in church who sings off-key because it means I can hear

☐ weariness and aching muscles at the end of the day because it means I have been productive

☐ the alarm that goes off in the early morning hours because it means I am alive

A Tour Director Tells Tour Stories

Foreign travel has become common for Americans as. . . well, domestic travel. In recent years, instead of taking the family car for a two-week vacation out West, ending in Yellowstone Park, travelers are just as likely to take that big shiny jet-airliner across the ocean for a couple weeks to Europe. Lots of going overseas by lots of folks. Initial planning for foreign travel requires the decision on either joining a group on a planned tour or going it alone, that is upon arrival in the overseas airport, get your rental-car and go when and where you want. First-time travelers tend to join a planned-tour group, the main reason being that everything is taken care of for them, transportation facilities or hotels or meals or side-trips, or whatever. With the planning and preparations all done for the tour group, the primary obligation as a member is simply to be on time because as most Tour Directors will inform them, especially on bus trips: "When one person is late, the whole group is late."

People ask me: " How many times have you been to Norway?" And my answer: "I'm not sure." This response is less to dodge the question than to indicate honestly that I've been there enough times to have lost count, not that the number is that large. The figure is somewhere over a dozen times but not more than twenty, and whatever the figure is, three-fourths of those trips have been as a Tour Director, either to Norway alone or a trip to all the Scandinavian countries. Either way, they're all memorable trips, some more memorable than others.

Like all jobs, there's both good and bad about being a Tour Director. The good part starts with just traveling to and through the Scandinavian countries; they're all great! As to the bad part, well . . . that depends on what the tour group is like. Before leaving, we're told to expect at least one "pill" in the entourage; it's true. Alas, for that unhappy person, nothing is ever right, never good enough. They say they're sorry they ever came along; the Tour Director is sorry too. (Such a person, when sentenced to be hanged, would complain if he/she weren't hanged with a new rope.)

And as to problems beyond anyone's control, there are several, starting with The Weather . . . (Tour Directors pray for sunshine and warm days . . . with rains coming only at night . . . and P.S. Lord, may no tour member get (hospital) sick . . .)

What To Worry About? Take Your Pick

Amid everything on every tour day is the constant concern about things not going right, things like buses and guides and speakers not showing up at all, let alone on time. To illustrate: In coming back late at night from a boat trip outside of Stockholm, there was no bus there to meet us and take us to our hotel. What to do? Well, round up a few taxis for some; the rest of us walked back, the distance being considerable but not overwhelming.

There's always the niggling feeling each traveling day of learning that your booked hotel is not booked at all when you show up with your tired group at the end of a long day. Are your vouchers—those payment slips and tickets and passes—there waiting for you the day you arrive? The day we arrived in Bergen and were to take a Fjord-Tour and all the folks lined up on the wharf to board the ship, the man taking the tickets indicated in very clear English that our tickets were invalid. What to do? Make some fast phone calls and HOPEFULLY get things straightened out at least quickly enough for the group to be allowed on board. The details of the snafu would come later. We made it on.

And looming over every day's activities is the perennial problem of illness. People on tours often get sick, sometimes very sick, sometimes critically-ill-sick, which leads to a cynical joke told only among Tour Directors, starting with their definition of a Good Tour: if you return home with the same number you left with. That's good—if rather sick. A tour director's admonition might be, "You cannot die over there! It's too complicating. Wait until you get home for your demise." Sounds both hard and glib, and maybe heartless, too, but it's true; dying in a foreign country produces an extended red-tape mess beyond all the obvious family anguish. Amid the agony are lots of long-distance phone-calls and decisions to be made quickly. For example, the directly-involved families, who had never even considered cremation, usually become quick converts after Q&A with overseas embassies.

> *... starting with their definition of a Good Tour: if you return home with the same number you left with.*

Starting Out; How Not To Do It

Tour Directors can screw up easily, especially if they're new at it. On my first tour, we took one of the Last Great Train Rides still available in Europe on the Oslo- Bergen run. It's an all-day scenic ride in which you start at sea level and end up at sea level on the other end, in between the Oslo Fjord and the North Sea. Those railroad cars go up and up so high in the mountains that you see glaciers below you and the terrain outside the windows looks like the surface of the moon. And then there's all those snaky track-turns in the mountains that are at times sharp enough for someone in the last car to see the engine in front broadside.

Anyway, we had the tickets for our group as we boarded the train to start the grand run, but we did not have assigned seats in assigned cars. Someone (me) had overlooked this necessity. A big screwup. The result for our group the rest of the traveling day was a form of "fruit-basket-upset" in that our folks would take a train seat, settle back to enjoy the ride, only to be informed after the next train stop—with new passengers getting on—that we were sitting in somebody's assigned seats. So move! We did. We learned.

Screwups In Copenhagen

Our train in Sweden was heading for Denmark and as we neared the water-border we were informed to just sit tight, that all the cars would get on a large ferry and cross the narrow straits from Helsingborg to Helsingør and from there it would go directly on into the Danish capital. And then oops, there was a change: almost all passengers were told to get off the train and walk through customs at the border, then get on a ferry boat to the mainland at which point we would again go directly to a train for the final leg into Copenhagen. However, for those few travelers for whom this would be difficult, they could stay on in one car that would go on a ferry and that car would be waiting there for the rest to join them for the final leg. Seemed simple; it wasn't.

In our tour group was an older and agitated man who had a major heart condition, so his wife convinced him to stay on this one car and wait and relax there before she and the rest of us would join him on the other side. He agreed, but reluctantly; he did not want to let her out of his sight. She was not that pleased about this arrangement either. Two very nervous people.

Anyway, the rest of us walked slowly—stop, step-step, stop, step-step—through customs, then boarded the ferry, headed for the Danish coastline and upon arrival we walked immediately to find and board our train. Except no train. And the car that had been a part of it was not there either. That special car had been attached to another train which was already on its way to Copenhagen when we arrived. Where was our man with the heart condition?

Taking a different, later train, our ride from Helsingør to Copenhagen took less than an hour but the trip went agonizingly slow for those of us who were ourselves now upset as to how and when and where we'd find the missing, agitated—and likely worse—husband with the bad ticker. Upon arrival, our first revelation was: That Copenhagen Railway Station is BIG! It took some time and lots of questions and lots of frantic running around to locate the car on which the missing husband had ridden. At last we found it. But he was not there. Where'd he go? How can we get a message to him in this huge station? Although announcements occur with regularity over the loudspeakers in that cavernous railroad station, getting anyone to make the announcement you want can be a hassle. The Danes behind the information-desk were not the least concerned about a single missing man, regardless of any medical problems. Hence no announcement, we were sorry to learn. The Danes seemed not the least bit sorry.

A quick strategy session among those of us most directly concerned included the option of checking the hotel where we'd all be staying as it was near the station (maybe he walked over there) so I agreed to make that check, made the fast-paced walk, got to the hotel and sure enough, I had just walked through the main entrance when I saw the missing man coming down the hall. That was the good news; the bad news was that he kept falling down. He'd get up and take a few more steps and then fall down again. At that exact moment there were two men with a heart problem. Finally—and it was not easy—we communicated enough for him to calm down a little and realize that all was at last OK, that his wife would soon be joining him and that he could go to his room and rest and relax. He did; when she arrived, we did too. And we all survived. No call to the American embassy. Whew!

Topless "Little Mermaid" Topped Out By Competition

The most famous symbol of Denmark in general and Copenhagen in particular is The Little Mermaid, that small statue of the maiden/mermaid sitting on a rock in the harbor, the city skyline of Hans Christian Andersen's home in the distance. No tour bus ever misses stopping to see the statue. It's a must see. The walk from the tour-bus to the shoreline is only a few yards and the response heard most from first-time viewers of The Little Mermaid is: "But it's so small." The statue is small and therefore often disappointing, at least to our group, whose members mumbled sweet nothings about being disturbed from their bus-nap for "only that." Feeling underwhelmed, they lumbered back to the bus on this beautiful, warm July day, then settled back for more anticipated boring sites and sights.

However, the bus had hardly traveled fifty feet farther when someone near the front exclaimed: "Look over there! Wow! Hey, ya gotta see this!" What they "gotta see" were about a dozen or more college-age girls lying on their backs sunbathing, and all were topless. This scene immediately found every passenger quickly moving as close as possible to the windows to stare, so many bodies on one side that the bus leaned dangerously and the driver pleaded for all to return to their seats. After the bus-buzz-buzz that followed the gawking, there was no sleeping; maybe there'd be some more to see . . .

"The Little Mermaid" in Copenhagen
. . ."it's so small" say the tourists . . .

Nudity and/or near nudity is common in Scandinavian countries. Citizens there seem to fit the category of Sun-Worshipers; and while sun-bathing, strip way down; the less on, the better. At the beaches—and at public fountains—it is simply standard for all the little kids to play and swim in the nude. And nearby there may be topless adult women lying sunbathing on the sand beaches. And all Scandinavia has their nude beaches. Ho hum, the usual on a nice sunny summer day in Scandinavia for skinny-dipping.

But nudity of any kind is not common for American tourists who visit Scandinavia. Indeed, viewing the superb statuary of sculptor Gustav Vigeland at Frogner Park in Oslo should be an aesthetic delight for any tourist, but it was not always so for some of our Americans who were not only surprised but appalled that every statue there in that huge park is a nude. (Good thing we did not have a Savonarola in our group.) But Oslo and all of Norway is prudish compared to Denmark. For example, walking around the shop-ping-block near the Copenhagen Railroad Station one finds ongoing front-window-displays of hard-core pornographic pictures and materials and supplies, all for sale, the likes of which can curl the hair of American philistines. While American eyes pop at the porn, the local citizens seldom give these shop-windows a second glance. Ho hum. Same old, same old . . .

Last Minute Searches For Lost Airplane Tickets ——

Prior to e-ticketing, airlines awarded paper-tickets to each passenger who, prior to boarding the plane, must have that ticket in hand to receive a boarding pass. No ticket = no getting on the plane. That simple. Naturally tour directors direct their group members to carefully store their tickets in a safe place where they can always be found; naturally tour directors implore their members the day before their plane leaves for home to have their tickets on their bodies the next morning on that last ride to the airport, and naturally there are a few who may hear well but do not listen to one single word.

When and if directors learn several days before takeoff that someone's tickets are "misplaced," a solution can usually be worked out with the airlines—or the missing tickets found—and it's less of a problem. However, it's upon learning about the missing ticket just as luggage is being checked in for the flight to America that there occurs An Immediate Problem.

An elderly woman in our group waited until the very end before letting me know that she couldn't find her ticket. She kept thinking it would turn up somewhere, somehow, that morning, and besides she didn't want to worry me. Within seconds of this revelation, my wife and I were just outside the airport entrance doors wildly distributing the contents of her two over-filled suitcases as we searched for the missing ticket. The frantic efforts—amid flying pajamas, socks, underwear, hair-curlers tossed on the sidewalk around us— was egged on by the PA system announcement that the boarding of our plane for America would begin in five minutes. So keep hunting faster. Keep throwing. Keep hoping. And then there it was! The ticket had been stuck inside the cover of an Ibsen book. Yay! But no

time to celebrate. Back in the suitcases went the stuff strewn on the sidewalk, jammed in as we rushed in just barely in time for the three of us to make it for boarding. (Extra pleadings helped.) The very last ones to enter the plane's cabin and walk down an empty aisle, a few of our group looked at us strangely and inquired why we were so flushed and harried. We just smiled. The plane ride home was very relaxing.

Thrills At Every Hairpin Turn

Driving in the Norwegian mountains—and it seems that Norway is mostly mountains—provides thrills for all tourists, some of them of the heart-stopping variety. Cars Way Up There on those narrow mountain roads, often without any guard rails for protection, can provide their drivers with instant white knuckles because when they take a peek Way Down There, they see only a surreal serpentine road that snakes back and forth all the way down the steep mountainside, and at the bottom can be picked out these tiny specks that are really big houses. A LONG way down. Prepare for hyperventilation. And hope the brakes work.

What adds instant energy to the vertical quagmire is for the driver to ease around a blind hairpin turn at the top of the mountain and there suddenly meet a bus. Uff da. Just meeting another car anyplace on a high mountain road requires each driver to come to a near stop, then proceed oh so slowly and oh so closely to the other car, the paint-job of each vehicle in danger of being scraped. But meeting a bus usually requires the car driver to stop, back up and up (or down and down) until finally finding a small turn-off-area carved into the mountain-side just for that purpose, there to squiggle the car in and wait for the bus to roll past before the driver dares return to the road again.

Many Americans have enough trouble trying to back their autos into a parking space at the local mall. Consider the concern of the driver backing a rented auto down a Norwegian mountain road (20%

grade), maneuvering/creeping around blind corners, until a turn-off cleft in the rock appears. That's stress.

Norsk bus drivers are excellent, the safest of safe drivers on mountain roads, but they too provide their own thrills, not because of their driving but because of the road situations. Our tour group was leaving the tiny town of Geiranger—the village at the end of perhaps Norway's most famous west-coast fjord—on our way to Oslo and, of course, we had to cross over a high mountain. In the village we could look way up and see the top of the mountain to be climbed, see the winding road turning back and forth the entire route, and know in our hearts that we would make it safely in our huge bus with our wonderful driver. Nothing to be afraid of. And yet . . .

In our group were two sisters, both young and married, who for two weeks had left their husbands and families back home while they were off to see the best of Norway, and up to that location at Geiranger, they had enjoyed everything. Where to be seated on a bus for the best views on a mountain road remains debatable but there is little debate on where the worst seats are: the back of the bus. The sisters were in the very last seat. All initially went well as the machine began its long climb upward; at first they made delightful Ooos-and-Ahhhs as we climbed higher and higher and began looking back down from where we had started.

Their sounds changed as the elevation changed. It seemed that the bus driver drove as fast as ever around these multiple hair-pin turns and the Oooos-and-Ahhhs quickly changed to multiple bursts of Ohhhs and several exclamations of Oh My! Our driver suddenly seemed a crazy man as he wound his mighty machine up and around the steady steep and always steeper curves, the engine roaring loudly. What's he doing? What if the engine should fail? It was these curves that did in the sisters because when the bus made those twisting sharp sweeping turns, the back end of the bus swung way out beyond the road, giving them the perception and panic that they had left the road. They believed they were hanging out there in space and assuredly we would all at any moment fall down the

mountainside, bouncing and rolling all the way back to Geiranger fjord, which was down so far away as to appear just a tiny pond.

What to do for two sisters ready to implode? The obvious solution was of course not-to-look! But this was not that easy to carry out as they kept peeking between the fingers of their hands over their faces while gasping for breath and saying multi "Oh-Nos." So another suggestion. Now desperate, they finally they agreed to do it: they both lay down on the floor and stayed there. Maybe the bus would indeed fall down the mountainside but at least this way they would not have to sit up and watch it tumble. It worked. The rest of the trip went fine. When in doubt, hit the floor, unless, of course, you're the driver.

Mountain-driving in Norway continues to produce stories by Americans who've done it, but the Norwegians themselves offer plenty tales of their own, their amusing stories regularly finding Danes as the source of their fun. If Norway is about as mountainous a nation that can be found, Denmark is about as flat as can be experienced, which is why Americans who bicycle in Europe know where to go. Norwegian wags believe they're not overstating the fact when they say that the highest point in Denmark is where you're upstairs in a two story house and standing on the top of a step-ladder.

The geographical contrasts between the two countries is so great that the most common story told by Norwegians involves Danes who have come to Norway for the first time—and decide to take a car-ride over the mountains. Almost always these stories end with the Dane driving his car near the top of the mountain and by that point so scared, so terrified, so traumatized that he stops the car right there and will not move—knowing he can't turn around, knowing for sure that he cannot make himself drive any farther up the treacherous mountain road—that he then "freezes," his hands locked on the steering wheel. He sits there in a catatonic state, breathing heavily, his unmoving car in the front of a line, holding up the line of honking autos. This common occurrence, as the Norwegians tell it, requires a local citizen to leave his car in line, get out and walk up to the Dane's car and make the offer to take over the driving until they get down safely to the valley on the other side.

> *Stress, thy name is mountain-driving in Norway.*

As the Norwegians relate this common story, this offer has never been refused; the only problem at this point is to get the Dane's fingers unlocked and unwrapped from the steering wheel so the new driver can take over. Stress, thy name is mountain-driving in Norway.

How Long To Stay?

Always there's the question of how long to stay on your vacation to Scandinavia. My answer to this is Two Weeks; that seems to be just the right amount of time for most American travelers because by that time they've seen enough and have had enough of foreign countries; they're ready to go home. One week is not enough; it's too short a time and the hurry required to "see it all"—whatever that means—makes for an unfulfilled journey. Three weeks becomes too long; just as one can get "castled out" and/or "cathedraled out" in mainland Europe, in Scandinavia tourists can get "scenery-ied out." Also there comes—into that third week—a negative repetitiveness of many things that were at first welcomed and appreciated; but two-weeks-plus- later those same things are not only unwelcomed but disdained.

It can begin with little things, such as the bed-coverings used in Scandinavian countries. There there are no blankets or quilts or bed-spreads; no layers of any covers; there is only one form of cover on a bed and it's called a "dyne," which might be defined in the U.S. as a "feather tick." Initial responses heard from some group members to dynes were "How quaint"; "How different"; "How simple"; "What fun." And their lines just prior to returning home: "I can hardly wait to crawl under some real covers"; "Gimme grandma's quilt any time"; "Oh how I long to see my beautiful bedspread again—indeed, any bedspread."

Breakfasts (frokost) served in Scandinavian hotels are BIG! They're usually served buffet-style (koldtbord) and the buffet tables have many foods on them, some of which are big surprises to Americans, starting with fish-for-breakfast, plenty of fish and varieties of both the fish and preparation, e.g. pickled herring (sild), smoked salmon (laks); boiled halibut (kveite).

And cheeses (ost)! One separate table or one section of the buffet counter with nothing but cheeses of multiple varieties of shapes and sizes and tastes and colors, from the dark-dark goat-cheese (gjeitost) to the pale and hole-filled Swiss cheese (sveitsiskost). And those breads (brød)! As many kinds of heavy, grain-filled dark breads (and always cut your own slices) as there are varieties of cheeses, with only one kind not available: sliced white bread. And initial responses to the Nordic foods: "Oh how interesting!"; "What wonderful surprises for breakfast"; "I know I'm going to love this"; "Their breakfasts are so healthy." And their lines prior to returning to America: "If I ever see pickled herring on a breakfast table again, I know I'm gonna throw up"; "They even leave the heads on; this one salmon kept staring at me"; "Yipes, nothing but cheese and more cheese; no wonder I'm all bound up"; "I can hardly wait to have a peanut butter sandwich made with sliced white bread again"; "I'm just dying for an American hamburger."

You Know It's Time . . .

Our group had arrived in Bergen the day before; the next morning our tour began with a bus trip to Myrdal where we would transfer to a special-train for the short but steep train-ride down to Flåm on the Sognefjord, there to catch a boat for the return trip to Bergen. A wide-awake group this first morning; they wanted to see everything and miss nothing, and each turn in the road produced ahead for them one glorious scene after another of nature's loveliness, sights much appreciated by the travelers, several of whom enthusiastically commented that now at last can they see for themselves how extraordinarily beautiful Norway is.

Swinging around one corner, deep in a valley with a mountain beside them—with a wispy mountain mist high over the entire valley—the travelers came upon a view before them that was virtually breathtaking. It had everything. Down the steep mountainside came

Tour bus with sign in window of director
... *unspoken "message:" please don't die over here* ...

water cascading in white sprays from some half dozen waterfalls, the waters at the bottom becoming little trickling streams that went into culverts and under the road, flowing into the rushing river beside the road. Looking up amid the trees and the rocks, way up on the side of the mountain one could barely see a tiny farmstead, the bucolic scene complete with a few cows grazing there dangerously on the edge of the precipice. With necks craning from one side to the other so as not to miss these aesthetic wonders, the experience produced a group feeling of such wonder and a silence of awe. They were overcome with emotion. No one talked. Amazing. Norway's scenery can do that easily and regularly to first-time, first-day travelers.

Two weeks later, the day before the return to America, our same group was on the same bus taking the same route. There was the same spectacular scenery along the route, including that one valley that initially was so overwhelming. This second time, however, there was silence also but for different reasons; this time the quiet was brought on by weariness (half were sleeping) and boredom, the repetitiveness of the many landscapes having done their job ("if you've seen one waterfall, you've seen 'em all"). After two weeks of touring Norway they were "scenery-ied out." It was time to go home.

There's No Place Like (Landing At) Home

The old adage about never missing anything until its gone applies also to overseas travelers. Among the many things most Americans seldom think about is their citizenship. It's just there, sort of like the air we breathe. And then an overseas trip brings the whole topic to the forefront, often for the first time, and with it comes a sudden appreciation of America, that borders on reverence for our country, our home. Nationalism lives.

While overseas with tour groups, I've on occasion heard folks talk about Americanism but not directly. It comes out mainly as folks begin to make comparisons—to differences, to the way things are in Europe compared to . . . well, things back home. At best this subtle patriotism is understated if stated at all that we've got it pretty good in the good-ol'-U.S.A., regardless of our many problems.

The overt, physical response to living in—and returning to—America, comes out regularly when the tour group flies back to the U.S after two weeks in Europe. We both saw and felt it when that big airplane we've been flying in for some seven hours over that big ocean begins to drop down below the clouds, when land and sometimes landmarks could be seen way down below, when the huge jet angles steadily downward for miles, prior to making its final approach and the long-awaited landing on the runway. It's in those last few seconds before the tires touch the earth that the passengers are so quiet; it's those few seconds just after the plane touches the tarmac that the passengers become so noisy. The spontaneous noises reveal the sounds and the voices of happiness, of satisfaction, of appreciation, all expressing the same thought: We're home! The great feeling of being home safe and sound is almost palpable among  passengers, and at that moment passengers often break forth in applause. Exactly what they're applauding is hardly clear. Whatever, certainly no one has told them to do this; no one has to tell them. It's automatic, it's visceral; it's the most wonderful feeling in the world to be home again.

The end is near (of the book, of course)

Surprises (Mostly Pleasant) in the Cemetery

Among the silent surprises of growing older are going back to your hometown and visiting the local cemetery and wandering among the many headstones. There's a quiet revelation. If one has been away for many years, the cemetery headstones silently inform you that you actually "know" more people in the cemetery than you do among the living in town.

Nothing like a cemetery as a good reminder about the facts of life, and death is a fact of life; no two people react to that reality of mortality in the same way. And since all of life is basically not mentioning "that thing"—that we're going to die—It's a topic to avoid. It's a little low on the list of subjects discussed at social gatherings. It's too . . . well, creepy ("HEAVY! No morbidity, please; let's change the subject"); so don't talk about it, don't think about it, and maybe it'll go away.

The mysteries around death and dying seem more upsetting to the young. For the old, however, the subject has been thought through at length and they accept it. Eventually comes a shrug, a nod, a sigh, a resignation of acceptance, and you move on from there.

And yes, of course, although death is often a shock, it's not often a surprise. It's just a normal and accepted phase in the cycle of life (and at times that cycle is short, alas); but such is nature and nature's God in operation. Simply accept—whether one is Buddhist or Lutheran—that those lines in Ecclesiastes are correct: "To everything there is a season . . . A time to be born and a time to die."

However, for Christians there's more; oh how there's more! Because especially in a cemetery is there the uplifting reminder that the term 'soul' should be considered with its proper theological definition: "The inner spirit of man that lives on after this earthly life." Therein lies the hope . . .

The Irony Of Living History

Cemeteries are a useful place to visit; indeed, a gravestone is a kind of outdoor history book. This town I write about was/is Scandinavia. The first immigrants began arriving in 1850, mainly from the region of Telemark in southern Norway. Consequently, all the different stages of Norwegian culture were lived and relived in America, starting with their Lutheran church (for a description and pictures of their first church—eventually the biggest church with the largest Norwegian Lutheran congregation in the entire U.S.!—see earlier book, Scandinavians Are Very Modest People, pp.16-19). Another carry-over in America was certain values; e.g., they valued almost nothing in life more than civility and stability.

The first immigrants began as true American pioneers in the mid-19th century. This meant hard times, a hard life. Way back then it was just another Midwest frontier community, a place where men were tough and often talked tough and prided themselves in their manliness. Many of their women folk were equally known for their earthy vocabularies and masculine accomplishments. They were —indeed, had to be—as a community, a strong people just to survive. From the evidence on the dates on the headstones in the Scandinavia cemetery, the majority of the male pioneers were in their 30s when they first arrived and they died in their mid 70s, a higher than average age for that time period.

The women might have shown the same longevity except that so many died prematurely in childbirth because childbearing was both a danger and a mystery, hidden behind taboos. When children were to be born, the menfolk alerted the community midwife and then the men left the house. This was women's business. In addition to bearing their children alone, many of the pioneer women were isolated in wintertime for two to three months a year when their menfolk went off to far away jobs in the logging woods. The women left behind with the children had to be strong to survive. For all these earliest families, it was a struggle.

Oh, Pioneers! We are your heirs and despite your hard times, The American Dream never ended in your community. You believed that if you worked hard and just kept going, a better day was coming, especially for your children and grandchildren. You were right.

The Commonality Of Headstones

The cemetery section for the oldest and first citizens can easily be spotted as their gravestones are almost all white-marble "tablets." These stones, standing (sometimes tilted) some three feet above the

ground, evoke the biblical (Hollywood?) scene of Moses and the Ten Commandments tablets. These once-white old gravestones/tablets are of course today more gray and sometimes black around the carved letters and dates, often making the letters indistinguishable, the names difficult to read. Yet deciphering those letters is worth the effort. Such wonderful old-world names— if difficult to pronounce—that can be illustrated only by listing a few, starting with the letter "A" and going only as far as The Andersons (the "Z's" are for the handful of Swiss immigrants in the area, like the Zwickys):

Gungild Aamodt, Osmund Gunnarson Aasen, Johannes Hanson Aas, Anlag Johannesson Mork Aanstad, Grete Abrahamsdatter, Theresa Larson Aekra, Matis Halvorson Akerhaugen, Bergit Lien Amundson, Andreas Bernt Anderson, Bendikka Aune Anderson, Ingeborg Gunn Andersen, Ole Severud Anderson, Margrethe Marte Anderson, Torkild Anderson, Sina Anderson, Rev. A.J. Anderson, et al.

Of note are only the initials for the "name" of Pastor Anderson, and it was the same for all the other Lutheran ministers of that period who did NOT want their full names known—even after dying—because first names might lead to an undesired familiarity with their parishioners and townspeople. No chumminess wanted. Certainly none of this first-name-stuff then with Pastors. This practice of Lutheran ministers using only their initials continued well into the 20th century; e.g. the Pastor who baptized me was the Rev. O.O. Sovde whom I never heard referred to by any other name than "Reverend Sovde." I never did learn what the "O.O." stood for.

Most of the gravestones of these earliest settlers had only their names, along with the years of their birth (født) and death (død). However, some of the oldest gravestones have reliefs showing two clasped hands, an allusion to a final meeting with God. Another common gravestone relief shows a weeping willow tree, certainly an appropriate metaphor, and of course the Christian Cross appeared on most stones. The words on almost all of the older stones were written in Norwegian, sometimes with misspellings both in names and quotations. The most common inscription carried the simple legend (in Norwegian): "Peace be with your ashes. Blessed be that memory." A sign of the changing times and passing decades (by the 1920s) revealed a curious combination of both English and Norwegian carved on the same stone.

There were variations inscribed about "leaving life's troubles behind." Among the most elaborate inscriptions is on the grave of one Niels Anderson Toldness who died in 1863 at age 61. It reads (translated): "Now I am contented/my heart is wasted seed/ to close my eyes/ and lay me down to rest/ though dust in its chamber/will rest now in peace/here life's struggles and laments/can never get you down."

It's enlightening and half amusing to contrast those 19th century headstones with those in the 21st century. By the year 2000, elaborate engravings of "pictures" has become common on many stones, sometimes with "pictures" showing the person's major interest or special hobby while alive, hence scenes of golfers, canoeists, fishermen, hunters, gardeners; a slough with ducks flying near decoys, their wings set. Animals and birds are very common today: bears, deer, eagles, dogs, cats, horses, loons. Also notable are outdoor scenes: lakes, fields, mountains, forests, farmsteads. Sometimes the person's vocation is pictured on the gravestone, e.g. musical-notes for a musician, a farm tractor, a power-shovel loading gravel in a dump-truck, a man climbing a telephone pole. Understandably, many changes between 19th and 21st century gravestones, but one common engraving somewhere on the headstones over the centuries—along with The Cross—is "flowers," whether shown individually or in bouquets. Certainly appropriate metaphors.

The Divisions

The Scandinavia Cemetery Association was incorporated in 1925 and arrangements made then and carried through to the present for perpetual care of the graves. Thus gradually removed were the low picket fences that once surrounded many of the older graves; all removed in order to facilitate maintenance. Mowing around head-stones can be a problem; picket fences made it even a bigger mowing problem.

The cemetery is divided into three sections, the oldest (above) obviously for the oldest graves, roughly encompassing the years 1850-1900; the second take in mostly the years 1900-1950; and then there's the "new section," the years since 1950. (Understandably it's not that neat a separation, there being scattered sites, for example, of someone who died in 1888 next to a 1988 grave.)

It's in this "New" section that I "know" so many of the persons laid to rest there. And making an annual trip to visit this place for over 50 years, I kept "knowing" more people every year. Each recognized name conjures up a recognized face along with a recognized line of identity going with it: "Hmmmm, there's Telford Torgerson, the Torgerson one-room Country School just down the road was named after that family." And there's my high school classmate, Allan Moe (1931–1960); "What a tragedy; how sad he lived such a short time." And then there's sites and sights that really give one pause: There's my folks' graves . . . and next to theirs is the stone of my only sister Madelyn (1920-1983) . . ." But what really gets the head nodding in recognizing and accepting one's own mortality is seeing your own gravestone on your own plot, a stone we had arranged to be placed on our site plenty early, but with no real interest in using it soon.

What should/should not appear on a headstone? Well, as usual, it depends . . . Picture engravings aside, almost all the wording includes just The Basics—some combination of "years on earth, marriage dates, wife's maiden name, parents of . . ."—and that's about all. A few try for more, a final closing line, even if summing up a lifetime in a single line is impossible. However, summing up a response to that life is possible, and so my wife Judy and I have added a few words which we think are appropriate; it's a simple phrase in Norwegian now engraved at the bottom of our gravestone which reads only: TAKK FOR ALT (Thanks For Everything).

After-Words For The Readers

A bit of fatalism accompanies us all in later life as we grapple to understand our own experiences in particular times and places and with particular people who talked and behaved in particular ways. But that's everyone's life. Where you grew up and how you grew up are part of your identity and it doesn't go away. It's who you are, In my case I've been lucky enough to write about many of those experiences and persons. However, this is my last book in this six-book series on Scandinavian-Americans and most likely the final book that I'll ever write, so I'd like also to add that same Norsk valedictory phrase to my readers: Takk For Alt.

(A tell-all) postscript

The Road to Writing
The Joy of . . . Writing

Some people get great joy from working crossword puzzles. Some people like to cook. Or paint. Or walk. Or run. Or nap. Or do nothing. Many others get equal joy and then some—certainly here in the Upper Midwest—from hunting or fishing—or any outdoor activities. Even camping: Ah, the call of the not so wild.

I like to write. I like words. I like books. I like dictionaries, and still have and still use the same dictionary I bought when I was a freshman at Luther College in Decorah, Iowa, back in 1949. (Actually my roommate and I bought this dictionary together, but I bought him out by year's end as he was well on his way to majoring in Extra Curricular Activities and minoring in Sin. He flunked out by June lst.)

Words took on special meaning in college because of the opportunity to write for the college newspaper. It was fun. At times exciting. And controversial, but always great schooling. I learned more in my association with that tiny newspaper than all the formal classes together—which is grudging admission that I was not the best Social Studies major in fly-away-Ioway.

By my senior year I was the co-editor of the newspaper and wrote a weekly column called 'The Headless Norseman.' It was read by all, but not appreciated by all. No surprise. Lesson learned early: you can't please 'em all. One learned the power of words, once so powerful that I suspect I'm one of the few college kids whose col-

umn touched the heart-and-mind of a local Lutheran Pastor to the point where he stormed into our newspaper office, waved the newspaper and waved his fat pointer-finger at me and declared in a stentorian voice that I would be going to hell unless I altered my purple prose! Hey, all I wrote about that week was this new discovery for the use of the belly-button: It's a good place to keep salt while eating celery in the bathtub. My my my. Threatened to perdition for that?

But maybe I shouldn't have added in the same column the revelation of this "recently discovered" poem titled ANTLERS IN THE TREETOPS by Who-Goosed-the-Moose. Ah, words words words at Luther College . . . Then again Martin Luther got in trouble for his words, too. (There's something a little weak in that analogy.) For samples of Headless prose, see pages 90-91 in REAL SCANDINAVIANS NEVER ASK DIRECTIONS. And one of the dumbest rhymes ever learned is what sticks and stones may do but words . . . always.

(Semi-irrelevant good news: words recently led to an unplanned barter system. A friend dropped by the house as I was working unsuccessfully on a plumbing problem. He looked it over and said, "There's nothing to fixing that." And he fixed it. Soon our conversation led to his admitting he was trying to write a book-report for an extension-class and had been working unsuccessfully on it. I looked it over and said, "There's nothing to fixing that." And I fixed it.)

Frustrations Amid Rejections

The oldest cliche among frustrated writers is their oft repeated lament: "It's not hard to write a book; what's hard is to get it published." That's true. Publishers each day receive unsolicited manuscripts by the hundreds in what they call "over the transom" submissions. Early on, with my faithful Smith-Corona, I joined the ranks of the thousands of writing-wanna-bees and ended up with a shoe-box full of form-rejection-slips. Boo hoo. Deflating, too. And there's another cliche among frustrated writers: "You can't publish nationally unless you get an agent and you can't get an agent until you've published nationally." Talk about a Catch-22!

(While attending a Sinclair Lewis Writers Conference, along with a couple hundred others, the overwhelming concern voiced by those in attendance was: "How do I get a book published? Huh? Please, tell me how . . .")

All of which leads me to first genuflect, grab my forelock, and then bow towards Cambridge, Minnesota, the home of ADVENTURE PUBLICATIONS, whose owners long ago agreed to publish my books, the first one back in 1977. It was titled—and I cringe now at those words—BROTHER HOTTENBOTTON. Bad. Really bad, Indeed, horrible. Titles are supposed to be catchy; Hottenbotton was ridiculous. Most people can't even pronounce it, let alone figure out what it was all about. There weren't that many readers interested in figuring . . .

Hitting The Jackpot

But ADVENTURE did well with the next one, THE LUTEFISK GHETTO: Life In A Norwegian-American Town, which came out in 1978 and was reprinted over and over again and 30 years later it still remains in print at this publication date, 2008. That book seemed to touch a special nerve among readers, the nerve that actually causes readers to write a letter to the author. That's rare. There was an overall response in their many letters which said in many different ways: 'What you described was my town; the only difference was that ours was primarily made up of . . . Swedes/ French/ German/ Finnish . . . otherwise the characters in it were very much the same.' The most eyebrow-raising letter came from a lady who wrote to say that she had read GHETTO six times, each time taking the book to bed with her along with a fresh bottle of red wine.

And one lady wrote upon finishing GHETTO: "Shame on you! How dare you toy with my affections that way! That ending . . . well, I was so disturbed to the point of being unable to sleep that night. And it was all your fault!" (Maybe she's the one who should have had the wine bottle.)

The GHETTO book led to a request to write a monthly column for a Scandinavian-American-Newspaper out of Fargo (no longer published). These columns mounted to the point where Adventure Publications was again approached and said to Go Ahead and the result was LEFTOVER LUTEFISK (1984), and not that long after that, LEFTOVER LEFSE (1988).

An Attempt To Explain Content

Of note are the titles of these books. The words are deliberately shouting to any potential reader standing there at the bookstore shelf, pawing and poking and riffling through one book after another, half-wondering what they're about. Well, THE TITLES TELL YOU THEY ARE ABOUT SCANDINAVIAN-AMERICANS. That's it; that's all. They're not love stories, nor mysteries; no unrequited romance in them, let alone s-e-x; they're not fiction, not made-up characters doing made-up actions; not some skinny middle-school novel on life-destructive zits. Ooops, as to "skinny," that's a deliberate decision too in the size of these S-A books because a book can't be too skinny and certainly not too fat. If there's a choice, err on the side of skinny-ness so as not to scare off any reader whose interests in books lean to lean. (Among my "scare books" is a history of Bemidji State University called UNIVERSITY IN THE PINES. It's 541 pages long! More than anybody ever cares to know about that school. Enough in shear volume and weight to scare off even the most devout alumni! Somehow the book never made it on the best-seller list in the *New York Times*. Oh well, but it makes a good doorstop.)

Then There's The Order

Which stories should go where? The order of the stories is deliberately chosen in all these Scandinavian books to add variety for the reader throughout the book, be it in the length of the article or the nature of the story—and tossed in among all are short-stuff- fillers, mostly there for fluff and fun. The intent/order/layout—indeed, the whole book itself—is the author trying to capture and reflect life itself. He believes that virtually every day for every one, even Scandinavians, there's the good and bad, funny and sad, informative and interesting and sometimes poignant episodes—amid the boring and blah days (alas, much of life is mundane and boring; same-old-same-old). Thankfully, I hope, there's enough uplifting stories along with some sad things—and some sections are just information; "just history." Confession time: Critics note, and alas I agree, that overall my books are often didactic (I too looked it up in my dictionary); I blame this on the school-teacher in me. Was I yet another victim of the pedagogical truth: those who can, do; those who can't, teach?

Finally, On To The Last Three Books

The owners of ADVENTURE PUBLICATIONS, Gordon and Gerri Slabaugh, chose to alter the format of my last three books, starting with *Real Scandinavians* Never Ask Directions (2000). Understandably, to each his own, and as "owners" they decided to do away with the line-drawings used in the first three books. Hence the covers—and inside illustrations—are very different but at least/at last these covers have attractive colors. And inside are little scattered 'pictures' illustrating something in the story; there are also boxed quotations taken from the article and the intent of both is to make the pages more attractive and inviting to the eye. Publishers understand "make-up." (Writers think they do but don't.) Indeed, it was a clever ADVENTURE employee who did the cover for *Scandinavians Are Very Modest People* (2004), which cover shows a statue of David dressed in shorts and wearing a Norwegian sweater.

And now we come to *Scandinavians Never Gossip—So Listen Carefully*. At this writing (December, 2007) I have no idea what that cover will look like. I expect to be pleasantly surprised, knowing that it will be good. Lots of surprises connected with this last/current book. It took only a few minutes to get the juices running again; get the joy rolling; get ideas roiling; get the fun back at the keyboard because honestly, there is THE JOY OF WRITING. It makes one come alive.

About the Author

Art Lee's interest in things Scandinavian came understandably and naturally, having been born, raised and schooled in a Norwegian-American town named Scandinavia, Wisconsin, and three of his four grandparents were emigrants from Norway.

Later in life, Art went to Norway and "saw where it all started" when he visited the exact place—the house, outbuildings, and tiny farm—from which his emigrant grandfather left in order to reach his Vesterheim (Western home) in the U.S.

He recommends such a trip to all Americans interested in their heritage, as this helped him come full circle with that fuzzy notion called "American-Norwegianess," if there is such a word.

And just as his grandfather emigrated from Norway to Amerika, his daughter married a Norwegian citizen and "remigrated" from America to Norway and has lived there (in Grimstad) for the past 17 years, with her husband Bjørn and their two boys (at this writing, ages 11 and 15.)

So why did/does the author write about things Scandinavian in general and Norwegians in particular? Because his college freshman English teacher told him to write about things one knows, and so he writes about plain small-town folks as they relate to each other, their heritage, and their community.

A retired history professor, Lee believes that history is too often thought of as a dry subject that's always about Presidents or

Politicians or Wars or Tariffs with too many dates to memorize. Not so, says Lee; "History is about people." And while the Big Histories concern themselves with the changing patterns in civilizations, it is the Little Histories that affect and interest most people. Relationships: That's Real History.

And it's easy to see Real History all around us; after all, the unintelligible prattling of his grandsons in Norwegian doesn't sound much different than the old men spouting Norsk on Main Street three generations back. Hearing this brings back the sounds that remind Grandpa of his own childhood, and it's easy to connect the past with the present in many ways. And when you think about it, the men outside the hardware store and his grandsons share something else besides a common language: Lee can hardly understand a word they are saying; THEY ALL TALK TOO FAST!